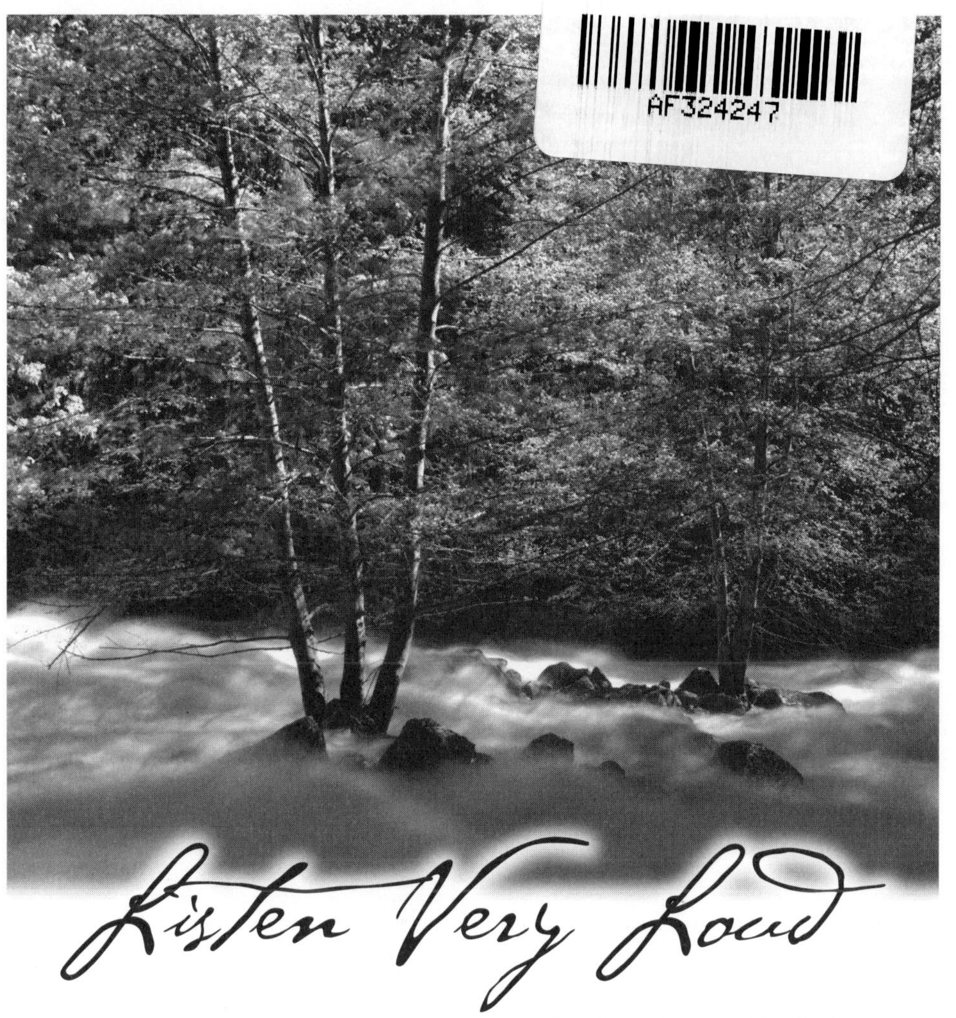

Listen Very Loud

by Randy L. Mitchell

PAYING ATTENTION in the STUDENT AFFAIRS PROFESSION

Listen Very Loud:
Paying Attention in the Student Affairs Profession
by Randy L. Mitchell

© 2001 by Atwood Publishing
2710 Atwood Ave.
Madison, WI 53704

Printed in the United States of America

Cover and text design © TLC Graphics, www.TLCGraphics.com

Library of Congress Cataloging-in-Publication Data

Mitchell, Randy L., 1954-
    Listen very loud: paying attention in the student affairs profession /
Randy L. Mitchell.
        p. cm.
    Includes bibliographical references.
    ISBN 1-891859-35-8
    1. Student affairs services--United States. I. Title.

LB2342.9 .M59 2001
378.1'94--dc21

                                                                2001018209

In the age of information,
we're losing our capacity to pay attention.
This book is about paying attention
in the student affairs profession.

Table of Contents

Foreword

If there's one thing that all of us in student affairs can relate to, it is the brisk pace of the profession and the daily dose of unanticipated curve balls we face.

We may be the world's best list makers and task planners. We may be among the finest schedulers. But how often — despite our best efforts and intentions — do our days look something like this:

8:00 a.m. — Arrive at office. Grab coffee. Greet co-workers.

8:05 to 8:20 — Plan day's activities.

So far so good.

8:21 — Answer phone. Vice president is calling. She needs that office assessment report a week sooner than she'd thought.

8:22 — Scrap daily activity plan.

8:23 — Start editing (or writing) the office assessment report.

8:31 — Greet student who stops by your office. Agree to write a letter of recommendation for him — even if it **is** by the end of the day tomorrow.

8:34 — Back to your assessment report.

8:35 — "Ting — You've got email!"

8:35 to 8:36 — Wrestle with overwhelming urge to read message immediately.

8:36 — Cave in to urge and read message.

8:37 to 8:46 — Reply to message.

8:46 — Back to your assessment report.

9:36 — Rush to 9:30 committee meeting you forgot about. Apologize for your tardiness.

10:37 — Return to your office. Go through voicemail messages that came in while you were at your meeting.

10:40 to 11:05 — Return phone calls.

11:06 — Back to your assessment report.

11:07 — Stop working on your assessment report to "briefly" discuss a "personal issue" with another student who has dropped by your office.

12:20 p.m. — Send student on her way with your good wishes; feel good that you were able to help her.

12:21 — Back to your assessment report.

12:22 — Realize you're hungry. Decide to skip lunch and have a cold Pop Tart at your desk instead.

12:23 — Shut your door, in hopes of minimizing interruptions.

12:24 — Back to your assessment report.

12:33 — Phone intercom rings. Colleague asks if you'll look over his portion of the assessment report right away. You agree to do so.

12:34 to 1:00 — Make edits on colleague's portion of the assessment. Return it to him.

1:05 to 1:17 — Answer colleague's questions about your questions.

1:17 to 1:29 — Back to your assessment report.

1:30 to 2:33 — Attend staff meeting.

2:34 — Finally, a bathroom break.

2:37 — Back to your assessment report.

2:39 — "Ting — You've got email!"

2:39 to 2:40 — Convince yourself you won't be hoodwinked into reading message right away this time.

2:40 — Back to your assessment report.

2:41 — Read email message after all. "It could be important."

2:42 to 2:43 — Issue one-word reply — "Yes" — to as-it-turns-out routine email. Kick yourself for having caved again.

2:44 Back to your assessment report.

2:45 to 3:38 — Experience the joy of 53 minutes of uninterrupted writing and thought.

3:38 — Answer phone. Leader of the student organization you advise says the one-hour meeting that starts at 4:00 will probably "run a little longer than usual" today. "Is that OK with you?" she asks. "Sure," you reply.

4:00 to 6:19 — Attend marathon student organization meeting. Do your best to coach members through various personality "issues" within the group.

6:20 — Back to your assessment report.

6:21 — Realize you're tired, you're cranky, and you miss your family. Go home.

7:17 — Answer phone at home. The student calling is "sorry to bother you at home" but "thought you wouldn't mind just this once." You say you don't.

7:17 to 7:48 — Talk to student.

8:00 to 8:30 — Watch TV. Re-introduce yourself to family.

9:30 — Go to bed, exhausted.

Next day — Repeat.

Sound familiar?

While (hopefully) not every day plays out this way, as often as not our days in student affairs tend to look and feel like this one, leaving little or no time to think and reflect. Even those among us who would seem to have the most potential — and, indeed, almost an obligation — to lead and model balanced work lives in the field aren't able to do so. Examples:

- The campus wellness coordinator I interviewed for an article I recently wrote — who had skipped her lunch to talk with me, and who told me that she regularly skips lunch so that she can keep up with all of her daily tasks and duties.

- A former counseling colleague of mine who I never witnessed having lunch, in two years' time.

- Another former counseling colleague of mine who always ate lunch at her desk while catching up on her professional reading.

You no doubt know — or are — your own examples.

We student affairs professionals are a committed, dedicated, and caring lot — especially when it comes to helping the other people who surround us each day. But too often, we don't practice the balance we preach to others. We drop the ball on ourselves. We don't take very good care of ourselves. We often don't even **listen** to ourselves.

That's a big reason why Randy Mitchell has written this thought-provoking book, *Listen Very Loud*. He hasn't penned a "me-telling-you" type of book; after all, he's in this thing with the rest of us! Rather, he's come up with a "we" book — a means for all of us in student affairs to slow down, take a step back, think about what we're doing — and, especially, **why** we're doing it — and, hopefully, change the way we pursue both our work and our day-to-day lives.

Randy is what I would call a "practical thinker" or an "applied thinker." There are lots of people in this world who have good ideas. But there are far fewer people who also have the gift for developing useful strategies to put those good ideas into practice. This book is the **tool** Randy has developed to help himself and all of us in the field get our own attention — hopefully each and every day as we read one or two of the essays Randy has included in this volume.

As he did in his previous book, *Fables, Labels, and Folding Tables* (1999), Randy invites us not only to pause for a bit with his essays, but also to think and reflect as well. (He even offers several "Reflection" questions at the end of each piece, just to get us started.) The book is written in such a way that you need not read it all in one sitting. (In fact, it's probably better not to.) You don't even need to read it in its paginated order; you can jump in wherever you'd like, depending on your mood and the particular issues you're facing or wishing to consider.

I like to think of Randy's book as a tool I can always carry with me in my briefcase, just as I'd never leave home without my calendar, my business cards, and my bottle of water. I hope you'll treat the book in much the same way — for a tool you use to remind yourself to slow down and reflect is really no good to you if you don't have it near at hand.

It took Randy's little daughter quite an effort — a physical grabbing and turning of his head, as you'll soon find out — to help him understand what it means to "listen very loud." There's no way that he, I, or anyone else will be able to grab your head and turn it to get your attention (although I suppose professional conferences might offer some potential for this type of strategy). But this book will get the job done — both today and every time you turn its pages — so that you never lose sight of the "why" in this profession we all love so much. And, indeed, so that you constantly and consciously pursue that "why" for a few moments each day, alone or with your colleagues.

"Listen very loud" — and enjoy!

Peter Vogt
College Career Counselor (and Randy's faithful editor)
Eden Prairie, Minnesota
January 2001

Acknowledgments

"You know, a self-made man is truly shallow,

For he's no one but who he wants to be."

STEPHEN STILLS

All creative effort is in fact collaborative. A painter, a choreographer, a sculptor, a writer — all require influences and inspiration, without which there would be no creation.

I'm fortunate to have many inspirers and influencers in my life. This book is the result of their impact on me. It's a pleasure to *listen very loud* to the many people whose gifts have produced the metaphors and ideas you're about to read. Some of them are very close to me. Some I've never met, but their words still echo in my ears.

I work for a vice president who's also an author. In the spirit of "it takes one to know one," Dr. Mark Warner of James Madison University (author of *The Complete Idiot's Guide to Self-Esteem*) engages with me in dialogue and discourse that inspire me to think, to feel, and to wonder. His support and suggestions have been valuable to me in my work and in my writing.

Linda Babler, my publisher at Atwood Publishing, took a chance on me two years ago with my previous book, *Fables, Labels, and Folding Tables: Reflections on the Student Affairs Profession*. Her attention to detail, her supportive approach in working with an author, her suggestions for improvements, and her continuing encouragement have helped me understand and appreciate the publishing business at its best. She also linked me with Peter Vogt, an incredible editor who has the capacity to make my best material even better.

My daughters have taught me so much about how to be a father, and now they're teaching me how to be the father of college students — without cramping their style. One of them is interested in pursuing a career in student affairs — not to follow in my footsteps, but to place hers where they belong. Thank you, Chandra and Darci, for breaking me in (Lindsey, you'll get your chance later) as a professional listener. Thanks also for giving me the title for this book; your childhood malapropisms have enriched my language.

I draw on the thoughts, ideas, quotes, and sounds created by a number of songwriters, poets, authors, and full-time thinkers throughout the book. I've tried to diligently give them credit for their contributions where appropriate.

I'd like to thank Dr. Lee Ward of James Madison University for his part in developing the ideas expressed in "Responsibility and Freedom: Keys to Learning," and for the many ways in which he stimulates my thinking.

Finally, my thanks and appreciation go to the friends and colleagues who reviewed early drafts of this book. I've learned to *listen very loud* to the comments and suggestions of Ruth Burnham (Bucknell University), Linda Moore (University of North Carolina at Wilmington), Rick Larson (James Madison University), Chandra Mitchell (University of Richmond, Class of 2000), and my incredibly talented and patient assistant, Judy Marshall.

This book is dedicated to the memory of my colleagues and friends who are no longer speaking, but whose words still make me *listen very loud*. It is also dedicated to Deb, my favorite listening partner.

Why the Title, "Listen Very Loud"?

No, "listen very loud" is *not* a grammatically correct phrase — but there's a good reason I chose it specifically as the title and theme of this book …

It's an admonition one of my daughters came up with one time when she was talking to me and she didn't think I was paying close enough attention. She spoke loudly enough — but she also told me I needed to *"listen very loud!"* She even grabbed my face and turned it so that I was looking directly into her eyes.

She got my attention — and I trust that her profound request gives you a lasting mental image of what it really means to "listen very loud." It sure has for me.

This book contains several compelling reasons why student affairs professionals must *listen very loud.*

Who Should Read This Book?

Trying to decide if this book is really for you? You'll find that it's a good "fit" if you're a:

- New professional encountering some of the challenges inherent in the student affairs profession (*you mean I'm not the only one having these experiences?*).

- Seasoned professional engaged in generative activity and looking for some new angles on old issues (*been there, done that, got the scars to prove it*).

- Graduate student or prospective graduate student intending to pursue a career in student affairs (*after I graduate, life will be so much easier*).

Why Should You Read This Book?

Our lives are made up of stories and insights. Something happens, we think about it or remember it in a special way, the story or insight takes on significance for us, and we share it with others. Through reflection of this kind we learn about others, ourselves, and the world around us.

The student affairs profession has volumes of uncollected stories and insights dating back to the first college students who encountered academic support from faculty members, deans, or other students. These are stories and insights that chronicle the evolution of higher education in the western world — stories and insights about us. In sharing my stories, I hope your own reflections come to light. We make sense of our world and our profession through such reflections. They give us a common understanding of our experiences and connect us to other people who have similar experiences.

Like its earlier companion volume — *Fables, Labels, and Folding Tables: Reflections on the Student Affairs Profession (1999)* — this book focuses more on **why** we do what we do in student affairs, and less on **how** to do it. Where other books stress the rich theoretical underpinnings of our profession, I'm concerned about the philosophical foundations. My focus is on the humanity, not the operations, of student affairs.

The pieces in this book are my way of examining and transforming the humanity of the student affairs profession. The title of this book, *Listen Very Loud*, though not grammatically correct, is my admonition to student affairs practitioners that we have a strong obligation to pay attention — to our students, to our colleagues, and to our own still, small voices. (The first piece, "Listen Very Loud," expands on this point.)

I'm also interested in some of the qualities of our profession that seem to be missing from the literature. I believe we need new perspectives on responsibility, success, motivation, balance, grief, sense, grace (harmony, acceptance, goodwill), and joy as these concepts relate to student affairs. That's why you'll find these topics covered in the book.

By reading this book and considering the questions posed in each piece for personal reflection and group discussion, you'll have the opportunity to:

1. *Listen very loud* to your own stories and insights so that your work will have greater value and deeper meaning for you and those you work with.

2. *Listen very loud* to — and possibly reframe — the language we use, with varying degrees of effectiveness, in our profession.

3. *Listen very loud* to the lessons shared every day by your students and colleagues, so that you can become more resourceful, more skilled, and more knowledgeable about the needs and expectations of our profession.

How to Read This Book

One of the best things to come about through digital technology, particularly in the audio world, is the "random" button. In my car or with my home stereo, I can listen to an entire CD in the order determined by the artist, or I can push the random button and let the player decide the order of performance. I like a little serendipity, so I often opt for the "random" choice. Nothing's better on a long road trip than a multi-disc CD player with a random button.

This book has a virtual random button. You can read the book from start to finish if you like, just as you were taught to in elementary school. But you do have other options; you can also consider and enjoy the pieces individually and independently.

Music is an art that has taught me how to "listen very loud." I've been fascinated by the interplay of lyrics, rhythms, chord progressions, and improvisation since early childhood. Songs are metaphors laden with insight. Each piece in this book begins with a song quote from one of the songwriters who I believe give us great metaphors for our work. Your responsibility as a reader is to think of additional songs, books, films, or paintings that force you to "listen very loud."

This book is not a handbook for the profession, a checklist of essential habits or skills, or a dissertation based on statistical research. It is primarily a reflection on my personal experience, intended to help you reflect on your own personal experience. Each piece concludes with three questions for discussion or personal reflection. If other questions arise as you read or discuss, even better. In the Appendix of the book, I've listed categories of reflection questions, along with the pieces in which the questions appear. If you prefer, start with the reflection questions in mind, then select the pieces that set up the questions.

I hope *Listen Very Loud* inspires you to pay deeper and closer attention to the messages and lessons of your professional life. I also hope it becomes a tool for planning, training, and presentation as you work with the students and staff on your campus. I'm extremely interested in your comments, reflections, and feedback; please share them with me at akornwoods@cs.com.

Read and listen — and enjoy!

R.L.M.

How to Listen to This Book

There's so much the world can teach you
Listen very loud

Maybe someone's trying to reach you
Listen very loud

There's a whispering voice inside you
Listen very loud

There's a thought that's been denied you
Listen very loud

When you stop and pay attention
There are lessons to be learned
You'll be blessed with grace and wisdom
Far beyond what you have earned
In the age of information
Listen very loud

Give the gift of education
Listen very loud

Listen to the hopes and wishes
Listen to the doubts and fears
Listen to the lilting laughter
Listen to the troubling tears
Listen to the dreams and visions
Listen to the hidden pain
Listen to the joy and wonder
Listen to the sad refrain
Listen 'til you know you've heard them
Listen 'til you have no doubt
Listen, learn, and share the message
Listen, listen very loud

Listen Very Loud

> "Say it loud, say it clear;
> You can listen as well as you hear."
>
> MIKE RUTHERFORD

Listen.

Please listen.

LISTEN VERY LOUD!

This expression first came to me from one of my daughters, when she was much younger. At the time, she didn't think I was paying close enough attention to her. It wasn't enough for her to speak very loudly; she also wanted me to *"listen* very loud." She even grabbed my face and turned it so that I was looking directly into her eyes.

She finally got my attention.

I'm not the world's greatest listener. I do a pretty good job, one on one, with people in my office, but even then I'm not always concentrating on the words, emotions, and expressions of the person I should be listening to. I'm easily distracted by other noises: those around me and those in my own head. I'm generally too busy framing a response to really hear the message; I miss the verbal and nonverbal messages that accompany the words. In far too many instances, I completely shut down all of my auditory faculties and tune out altogether.

On the other hand, I love to talk. I've developed the capacity to articulate, to persuade, to illustrate, and to think out loud. I can get up and "say a few words" to an audience with little or no preparation. I can prepare a speech so that its length varies and it covers several topics. I lost my stage fright at an early age.

Unfortunately, there's a great deal about listening that I never learned.

Joyce Dowdall, president of the Generative Leadership Group in Somerville, New Jersey, believes we should engage in what she calls *generous listening* (2000, 38): "I don't mean just being more attentive. I mean taking listening further and fully receiving what another person is saying in a way that allows us to see something we didn't see before — the possibility of change. Listening this way becomes opportunity." Generous listening goes beyond the classic concept of active listening; it's not a matter of simply repeating what the speaker is saying; it's getting to the very heart and soul of what the speaker is saying.

Student affairs is a profession that requires us as practitioners to pay total attention and to engage our clients with generous listening.

If the last time you practiced generous listening was in a college-level counseling course, it's high time to refresh and renew your listening competency. Competent listening is much more than a set of skills: it requires not just the *skill* to listen, but the *will* to listen and the capacity to be still to listen; it requires capability as well as sensitivity.

It's no coincidence that, in Old English, the word for listen, *hlysnan*, is closely related to the word for loud, *hlud*. People from antiquity apparently knew what it meant to listen very loud. Do we?

We have many opportunities in our daily interactions with students, staff, faculty, parents, and guests to listen so that the other person will feel listened to. If we've personally been the recipient of this type of listening, we know how good it feels. I believe that it feels just as good to be the listener.

When I was a director of new student orientation, I had the pleasure of addressing the parents of college students at 12 successive orientation sessions each summer. My comments were filled with information, humor, and confidence. I was sure I was helping the parents relax a bit, communicating valuable advice, and portraying the aptness of the institution to anticipate and address every possible need or concern of its incoming students. When parents asked questions after my presentation, I was quick with witty responses.

I wasn't listening very loud.

One day, a colleague accompanied me for this part of the program. When a mother asked a question about campus safety, I was startled when my colleague didn't immediately answer the question — as I always did.

Instead, he acknowledged the question!

"I'm sure that's a great concern for you," he replied. "As a matter of fact, it's a concern for all parents. How many of you are concerned about campus safety?" Most of the hands in the audience went up. "We share your concern on our campus; so much so that we've spent a lot of time coming up with ways to address the concern. Let me share with you some of the ways we address campus safety."

At the end of the program, I'm sure that most of the parents in the auditorium had a much better sense of our approach to campus safety. Not because the program had changed, but because they believed that we'd listened.

Since that day I've worked much harder at acknowledging people's questions before attempting to answer them. Acknowledging the question validates the questioner, and it demonstrates that the listener is listening very loud. What do people want from us? Theologian and author Paul Tillich says, "They want us to listen. They want us to understand their intrinsic claims, their justice of being. But we can only give it to them through the love that listens." I've had to learn to listen with love — to the parents of college students, to students, to my peers, and even to my own still, small voice.

Competent listening requires the *skill* to listen. Develop your listening abilities, proficiencies, and talents through workshops, presentations, literature, video, and by consciously focusing on the words and messages you're receiving from other people. Then, practice listening. You'll be surprised to discover how easy it is to really listen, if you try.

Competent listening requires the *will* to listen. Develop your determination, your intention, and your resolve to listen very loud to the words and messages you're receiving from others. If you truly want to listen, you're positioned to use all of your listening faculties.

Competent listening requires the capacity to be *still* to listen. Develop your capability to turn off all other internal and external distractions so that you can be right here, right now. To pay full attention to another person — to "be here now" for someone else — is one of the best possible gifts that you can offer your students, your colleagues, and even yourself.

The *skill* to listen. The *will* to listen. The capacity to be *still* to listen. These should be considered essential competencies for the student affairs practitioner.

It's very hard to listen when you're talking; when you're emotionally charged; when you're creating a line of defense; or when you're knee deep in "administrivia." But if you listen very loud, you might be surprised to discover what James A. Autry (1991, 32) has already discovered for us:

> *Listen.*
> *In every office*
> *you hear the threads*
> *of love and joy and fear and guilt,*
> *the cries for celebration and reassurance,*
> *and somehow you know that connecting those threads*
> *is what you are supposed to do*
> *and business takes care of itself.*

REFLECTION

1) What do you need to do to improve your *skill* to listen, your *will* to listen, and your capacity to be *still* to listen?

2) Think of a situation in which you felt you weren't adequately heard. What could you have done to make sure the other person listened very loud?

3) What does paying attention mean to you, and how can it be applied to your work in student affairs?

Listen very loud to the lessons of your life.

"My father's hair has turned to gray now;
I never stopped to ask him why.
And all the things that he once treasured,
I see them slowly passing by."

JIM SEALS

Let me tell you about my dad.

It's important to me because I'm a dad too. It's also important because I think there are some lessons for the student affairs profession in the things — both good and bad — I learned from my dad.

My dad and I have many things in common, but I'm a different kind of dad than he is. That's understandable; we grew up in different worlds at different times. He grew up during the Depression, without a father; I grew up during the expansion years of the 1950s and 1960s, when anything seemed possible. His parents were divorced; so were mine. He served in the Army, then went to barber college; I skipped the service and got a master's degree in education. I think I look a lot like my dad, though it's somewhat disguised under the beard I've worn for the last 14 years. Still, I frequently see my father when I look in the mirror.

These, then, were — and are — my lessons from the Big Guy.

It's important to carry a song in your heart, whether or not you share it with the world. Once upon a time, my dad was a bear of a man, larger than life. He sang with all the verve and gusto of an old beer commercial. Hymns, Broadway show tunes, standards from the '40s and '50s; the source of the song didn't matter, nor did knowing all of the correct words. He broke into song at a moment's notice, like a character in an old musical, often to the surprise of whomever happened to be within the extensive range of his voice. A tendency to break into song at the drop of a hat and a voice that carries — these are qualities I inherited from my dad.

It might not be biologically possible to have a song in your heart, but we all carry the beat there even if we can't carry a tune. There are people in my office and on my staff — I'm one of them — who have the habit of breaking into song without warning. We've even created a group of faculty and staff who sing and play instruments — The Staff Infection — to perform at university picnics. We've chosen to share our music with the world; you can decide for yourself.

The point: Music and all other forms of human expression have the capacity to touch our hearts, our souls, and our minds, and they give us the opportunity to connect with others. Carry a song in your heart, and if you're lucky, you'll soon be harmonizing with others. Even if you can't sing or play an instrument, you can play the most important musical role of all: being an audience member. To carry a song in your heart, to marvel at the expression and emotion in a painting, to cry at the end of a movie, to be carried away in the pages of a good book — these are some of the ways we can know and appreciate the joy of human expression. Find your own way to carry the art of humanness within you.

Celebrate the seasons and passages of life. In the language of Charles Dickens, my father "kept Christmas." Through his own children he vicariously made up for the scarcities in his own childhood. The sights, sounds, aromas, and trappings of Christmas were abundant. Old-fashioned Christmas candy, a pile of presents under an angel-hair-covered tree, colored lights across the front of the three-bedroom ranch house, the obligatory game of Monopoly on Christmas day — Christmas was always a time of joy in my dad's house. That's another quality I inherited from him.

Celebrating the seasons and passages of our professional lives is just as important as the celebrations of our personal lives. We honor our growth through celebration. There are many opportunities for celebrations in the world of student affairs: The hiring of new staff. The beginning of the academic year. Fridays. Crisp fall afternoons. Homecoming reunions with former students. The day before a campus holiday. The return to the campus after a holiday, before the students arrive. The return of students to the campus after a break. Weddings and new babies. Successful conference presentations. Leadership recognition banquets. Commencement. The retirement of old friends. This list is intentionally incomplete; it's up to you to fill in what's missing.

The point: There is much to celebrate in our professional world, and it's up to us to seize the day.

You're never too old to act young; play is good for the soul. In the early years, my dad was famous in our neighborhood for showing up in the street in front of our house or in the vacant lot behind the house with a baseball and bat. "This one's worth a nickel," he would say as he tossed the ball up and took a swing at it. "There's a dime with your name on it if you catch this one" would be next. Nobody got rich, but I'm sure the neighbor kids' impression of my dad was primarily that he was a pretty swell guy.

My father also loved amusement parks. Our local choices in the Denver area were Lakeside and Elitch Gardens, two early twentieth century visions of diversion and entertainment. The child in my father who had to grow up too fast during the Great Depression got to come out and play when he took his family to the amusement park.

One of the greatest benefits of working in higher education is the potential for staying just a little bit younger than our real age. The professionals who think they can only be professional if they act their age are sadly mistaken. Youth and vitality are present on most college campuses — even those that serve primarily nontraditional students — and it takes strong resistance to keep from being infected.

But why resist? To be truly effective, we need to know what motivates our students. Student affairs professionals get to let their hair down just a little, loosen the tie or scarf just a bit, and remember what it means to be young and alive. Some of us do that by playing musical instruments. Some of us play golf, tennis, or other sports. Some of us play cards. Some of us also play the fool, the field, the odds, possum, hard-to-get, for sympathy, around, tricks, the lead, for keeps, dead, etc. We need to play to remain human.

Play is not the opposite of work. On a good day, some of my best work is play. On a bad day, it might just be a little playing that makes it all worthwhile. Play is where imagination, creativity, energy, wonder, and life come together in a meaningful, "wonder-full" way. We can teach our students a great deal by showing them that it's OK to keep playing after you "grow up."

You can't really see the value of "here" unless you've been "there." My dad's idea of a vacation was to drive until you drop. One particular vacation I'll never forget included Yellowstone; a visit to my grandmother's place in Olympia, Washington; a ferry cruise into Canada; a drive to Modesto, California, to see my grandfather; the family visit to Disneyland; a dip down into Mexico; then a beeline drive back to Colorado — all in about ten days. We saw a lot of country from a moving vehicle, but we generally returned home exhausted.

Perhaps my dad's form of travel only skimmed the surface; it's hard to get an appreciation for an area if you only experience it from the window of a passing car. Nonetheless, his wanderlust was passed on to me, and I've enjoyed exploring the world with a little more attention to depth and detail.

I've had the great fortune to travel extensively in my professional capacity. Much of this travel has occurred through site visits — seeing how other institutions address the needs of their students through innovations, renovations, new construction, and best practices. Additional travel opportunities have come about through regional and national conferences, seminars, and workshops. I generally come back with two significant realizations:

- There's a world of great ideas and great people out there, and you can learn so much by seeing this world firsthand.

- I'm blessed to work with great colleagues in a great job on a great campus in a great community.

Even if there's no place like home, you have to go someplace else to realize it.

Work, like life, is about relationships. During most of his productive work life, my dad served in a delivery capacity. He spent several years delivering dairy products before settling in as a postal carrier.

As very young boys, my brother and I occasionally rode along with our dad on his rural milk route. Long before mandatory seat belts, we rode in the back of the delivery truck, sometimes piling the empty milk crates as high as we could, then perching on them until they tumbled into a heap on top of us. It's a miracle we were never seriously hurt.

My dad was always friendly with his customers and they always looked forward to his daily visits. He knew all of them by name, address, and typical order. He knew their children, who had dogs, and which dogs were approachable. These people were much more than customers in my dad's eyes; they were his neighbors and friends. Long before anyone wrote a book or gave a speech on the subject, my father was practicing quality customer service through his relationships with his neighbors and friends.

The student affairs profession is built on the establishment and maintenance of effective relationships. To be effective, we must cultivate and nourish one-on-one relationships with individual students, faculty, parents, vendors, and other staff. There can be no success in our profession in the absence of strong, productive connections among ourselves and the many people with whom we interact on a daily basis.

Incidentally, you can't *have* a relationship of any kind; you have to continually produce relationships. Relationships require care and feeding; you have to cultivate and nurture them. Like living plants, relationships can't live without the warm sunshine of support, the cooling waters of care, the fresh air of understanding, and the invigorating nutrients of challenge. Ours is a profession of living relationships.

In your own way, whistle while you work. When my dad left the dairy and went to work for the post office, my brother and I were in school. I'm sure the pay and benefits of the post office were better, but the job to me didn't seem like it would be as much fun. Still, my dad had the reputation in town of being the whistling mailman. He told me once that he whistled because his back hurt so much, and the whistling took his mind off the pain. Even so, the whistling gave him a reputation in our little community.

There are certain people who always seem to have an extra bounce in their walk; others I know seem to be able to glide through a room as if their feet are barely touching the ground. These people aren't necessarily happier than anyone else, but their bodies seem to be speaking, as if to say, "I'm alive and life is good." A teapot or a steam engine lets off excess pressure by whistling; so can we. Through exercise, a midday walk, a phone call or e-mail to a friend or colleague, a short music break, or just a few minutes of quiet reflection, we can release excess pressure and get back on track. If it works for you, you might even try whistling.

The point: It's important in our work to find ways to let off a little steam.

Sometimes you just gotta move to what moves you. When my dad and mom were still together, they loved to dance. I truly believe it's why they got together in the first place. I never saw them dance in public, but every now and then my dad would crank up the blonde-wood hi-fi in the living room, generally to Glen Miller or Benny Goodman, and dance his version of the jitterbug with my mom. My brother, sisters, and I loved to watch his exaggerated movements; the whole house shook as he made his way across the floor. If you crossed Fred Astaire with one of the Clydesdale horses, you'd have a sense of my dad's style of dance. He had some smooth moves but his thundering hooves were the most dominant feature. I never learned to dance, but I remember watching my parents "cut a rug" (it was shag) in our living room.

I have a colleague from a nearby college who loves to dance. This guy has been active in several professional organizations for as long as I've known him, and I think I know his secret. Sure, he's great at committee work and providing leadership, but the real reason he makes these contributions and sacrifices is because, at the end of the day, *he gets to dance*! For someone like me with two left feet, he's poetry in motion. He'll dance with anyone — it doesn't matter whether or not he knows him or her — because he loves to dance.

People like him and my dad have taught me to do what you love. Sometimes you just gotta dance. Or sing. Or knit. Or paint. Or run. In our profession, we need to find what moves us, and then we need to move.

For many things in life, we should rely on others. My father was a lousy cook. I never had the courage to tell him that to his face, but the man just couldn't cook. Once in a while he would try his hand in the kitchen. His primary dish consisted of macaroni and melted Velveeta cheese garnished with saltine crackers. It was awful. I think it was a throwback to his Depression-era nutrition. He was proud of his meal, and we were careful not to upset him with our grimaces and difficulty in swallowing each bite.

He was much better at eating than he was at cooking, with an emphasis on meat (overcooked) and potatoes. Of course, the best meals took place not in our kitchen but at Colacci's, the authentic Italian restaurant in a nearby town. Life was pretty darn good when we got to eat at Colacci's.

Though he tried, my dad failed in his role as a handyman. He could handle small projects, but the big jobs got the better of him. One job in particular sticks in my memory. Dad had decided he would re-shingle the roof rather than have roofers do it. He indentured my brother and me to assist. We'd pretty much finished the front of the house before it occurred to him that we hadn't followed a pattern; wavy lines predominated. Dad chose to leave it as it was rather than take it all up and start again.

On the back of the house, with a pattern now in place, my dad set a large can of gasoline on the sloping roof for some reason. I can't remember which of us knocked it over, but it left a large stain where the gasoline dissolved the pigment in the shingle. The roof project was a do-it-yourself job, and everyone knew it. We completed the job, but it would have been much better with the help of experts. The lack of home improvement skills is yet another of my inheritances from my dad, but it's forced me to face up to my personal limitations and call the pros when I should.

It's my hope that the American myth of the rugged individual won't last another century. The rugged individual isn't very good at building community. The rugged individual limits himself or herself to his or her own capabilities, experiences, and knowledge. The rugged individual is self-serving. We need to teach and model interdependence as a higher good than independence. There are so many things I can't do; I'm blessed to be surrounded by colleagues, friends, and family members who *can* do many of those things. Similarly, none of our departments or offices on campus is self-sufficient; we rely on each other to realize the institution's mission. Moreover, when we rely on others, the results are generally much better than when we try to fly solo. We are the products of our interactions with others.

All of us are only human. I have plenty of memories of my dad, some pleasant and joyful, some confusing and sad. Sometimes he made mistakes and sometimes he made amends. Sometimes he showered us with love; sometimes his frustrations and temper took over. Sometimes he went out of his way to make us happy; sometimes we went out of our way to escape his anger. He wasn't perfect; he's just a man. And a dad.

We are only human, but we are fully human. We are humans before we are employees, supervisors, colleagues, leaders, or followers. Sometimes we hurt, get sick, change our minds, or have needs that conflict with those of the workplace. We make mistakes. We make amends. We make the best of our situations. We can't check our humanity at the office door; it's our humanity that makes us capable of relating to the rest of humanity. We have to relate to each student, parent, or colleague as a unique human being with unique human needs. Each person is a living, breathing, dreaming, worrying, thinking member of the human race who has an inherent worth and dignity.

To be truly professional we must be truly human, experience all human emotions, and relate to the humanity in others.

We have the opportunity to learn from the past. Many years have passed, and I have an increased sense of understanding for my dad. I had it pretty good. He grew up in an era without some of the benefits of medicine and treatment that we now can receive. He grew up with an absentee father in times of poverty and war. He probably did the best he could with the tools he was given. He has a history; so do I.

How well do you know the history of student affairs or of your particular discipline? Beyond graduate courses in higher education administration, what do you really know of your own professional roots? If we don't understand where we came from, it's difficult to determine where we're going.

Much of the discussion in recent years regarding student learning has come about, in part, because many of us in the student affairs profession have lost sight of our original function: to support student learning. In many ways, we've tried to become a separate academy of our own, the college of student development. It's good for the profession that we're rediscovering our original mission. Student development can be an important aspect of student learning, but it should not be seen as an end unto itself. We're a part of something larger, something more significant. In our profession, we need to understand where we've been in order to determine where we're going.

Honor your predecessors. There's no such thing as the perfect dad, or the perfect marriage, or the perfect job, or the perfect church, or the perfect neighborhood; humans just aren't made that way. My dad wasn't perfect, and neither am I. Time and distance take their toll on relationships. My dad is too far away for me to give him the kind of ongoing support I would like to give him. I forgive my dad for any grievances that might have come between us, and I hope he does the same for me. I love him as only a son can love a father.

Everyone I know in the student affairs profession can readily point to one or more individuals who influenced their decision to enter the field. Mentors and models regularly regenerate the profession through their influence, direction, and advice. Ours is not a very old profession, and it's possible to trace most of the people working today back through their mentors and models to a handful of student affairs pioneers. In effect, we're all related; we're first, second, and third cousins in the family of student affairs.

Unfortunately, like so much of modern American society, we know very little about our ancestors beyond the second generation. Perhaps we should do a better job of genealogy. In the meantime, honor your predecessors by thanking them, publicly and privately, for their influence. Recognize them by naming programs or facilities after them. Keep their memory alive by living their legacy. We have inherited a profession that others will inherit from us.

These, then, are my lessons from the Big Guy. Imagine what our campuses would be like if we practiced these lessons — and the lessons from each person's "Big Guy" — every day.

REFLECTION

1) What lessons from your predecessors could you apply to your work in higher education?

2) What are the lessons you hope to pass on to your children, your students, your staff, and your friends?

3) How do you intend to share your lessons with others?

   Listen very loud to the mentors and models in your life.

I'm Still Alive

"I've got great expectations, I've got family and friends
I've got satisfying work, I've got a back that bends
For every breath, for every day of living
This is my Thanksgiving."

DON HENLEY, STAN LYNCH, AND JAI WINDING

Listening to a National Public Radio broadcast recently, I heard an interesting story about a woman interviewing people who are over one hundred years old. She started out with a set of "big" questions for them but soon realized that her questions were on the wrong track. Her conclusion: Rather than asking people, "What is the meaning of life?" we should instead be asking them, "What gives your life meaning?" A subtle yet meaningful difference.

The story took on special significance for me because I had recently lost a friend to a long struggle with cancer.

Meg, like me, had spent most of her adult life in student affairs work. She'd held a variety of positions in student activities and student unions, from Missouri to Hawaii and, ultimately, to Utah. I first met her when she presented an educational session on staff evaluation at a national conference. Later I was fortunate to serve with her on the national conference planning committee that she chaired. The conference was held in Honolulu; in addition to serving as our fearless leader, Meg also became our island tour guide and social director. Though Meg lived in several different locations, I'll always associate her with the islands.

Meg was one of the graces of our profession, an ambassador of civility, dignity, goodwill, and good manners. She always made the best of her circumstances, both in terms of her stewardship and her leadership. She was one of the people who brought grace into my life — through the harmony, acceptance, and goodwill that she continually exhibited.

She was an exemplary professional, a runner, a wife, and a loving mother of two.

A couple of years after our national conference experience, Meg was diagnosed with cancer. It was hard for the rest of us to believe that someone so healthy and full of life could be riddled with cancer, but it was true. Most people in Meg's condition would have lasted less than six months. But Meg wasn't most people. She beat the odds through a combination of will, discipline, treatment, and resilience. She had high points and low points, but she was able to work intermittently and carry on her life.

The conference committee was able to gather in Los Angeles for a reunion a few years later at another national conference. We arranged a time to call Meg from the hotel. After the small talk, one of the women from the committee asked, "So how are you really, Meg?"

"I'm still alive."

Those three, simple words said so much. Three words that the rest of us take for granted every day.

At that same conference, a keynote speaker reminded those of us in the audience to seize the day. I decided she was right. My conference roommate and I left the conference, rented a car, and drove through Hollywood and Beverly Hills, ending up in a small bar on the Santa Monica Pier, sipping beers and watching the waves hit the shore. We were a coast away from my home, a world away from Meg's condition, thinking about what she had said.

"I'm still alive."

Mr. Keating, the teacher Robin Williams played in the film *Dead Poets Society*, takes his students down to the lobby of the school to look at the pictures of the long-departed students in the trophy cases. "Gather ye rosebuds while ye may," he tells them. It's a beautiful scene. In our daily trials and tribulations, we often forget to gather the rosebuds that lie all around us, or to model this important competency for our students. In the language of Stephen Covey, we focus on what's urgent, not on what's important. If we ever take the time to wax philosophic, we ponder "What is the meaning of life?" rather than the more important question: "What gives our life meaning?"

My friend Meg gave me a gift, one that will stay with me throughout my life. She demonstrated to me that we can choose life, as long as we're living. We have the opportunity in our professional lives to pass along this gift. As Don Henley sings in the song quoted at the beginning of this piece, "It's too long we've been living these unexamined lives."

Meg, my professional friend and colleague, passed away in early 2000. She was recognized and honored by her professional association. In tribute, I offered the following poem for the woman who let us play at the beach one day, many years ago, when we should have been doing committee work:

building a castle

a woman can stand alone in the sand,
building a castle by hand.
alone on the beach, the sea within reach,
building a castle with sand.

her hands are her tools, she follows no rules,
building is something she does.
the tide's coming in, the ocean will win;
building a castle because.

castles of sand are my gift to the sea,
although it expects very little of me.
footprints were never intended to last;
forever is mostly a thing of the past.
i'm building my castles with sand.

although the tide won't be denied,
building continues each day.
let the wind blow, let the waves flow
building a castle is play.

castles of dreams, illusions, and schemes;
building to help us survive.
castles to feel, demolish, and heal
building because we're alive.

castles of sand are my gift to the sea,
although it expects very little of me.
footprints were never intended to last;
forever is mostly a thing of the past.
i'm building my castles with sand.

a woman can stand alone in the sand,
building and breathing her art.
deep in her soul, a part of the whole;
building a castle by heart.

REFLECTION

1) What gives your life meaning?

2) What are some of the ways we can encourage our students and colleagues to examine their lives?

3) How can we most appropriately honor and recognize the peers we've lost?

Listen very loud to the people, places,
and purposes that bring meaning to your life.

The Hand of Grace

"These times are so uncertain, there's a yearning
undefined … people filled with rage
We all need a little tenderness,
how can love survive in such a graceless age?"

MIKE CAMPBELL, DON HENLEY, AND J.D. SOUTHER

I use my hands for many functions. They play the guitar moderately well and the piano less well but no less passionately. They have their own style of keyboarding on computers and typewriters; the best I could get in junior high typing was a D, but I'm one of the fastest three fingered typists I know. My hands have held the hands of my daughters and my wife; they've shaken the hands of countless others. Most of the time, my hands are instruments of grace.

Grace *is* amazing, just as the old Christian hymn exclaims. Perhaps that's why it's such a surprise when we actually encounter grace in our lives and in our work. For far too long we've relegated the word grace to the pulpit or, at the very least, to the dinner table. Yet grace can have a significant place in the rest of our lives, and particularly in our work in higher education.

Like a *grace note* — the type of note in music that need not be played, but that adds to the attraction of the piece — grace isn't required in our lives and in our work. But it certainly has the potential of making our lives and our work more meaningful. I believe we have a significant responsibility in student affairs to discover and communicate these moments of meaning for our colleagues and our students and ourselves. We need to be grace-full if we truly want to have a positive impact on our campuses, in our communities, and in our world. We need to be givers and receivers of grace "in such a graceless age."

What is grace? I imagine grace as an open hand with five fingers:

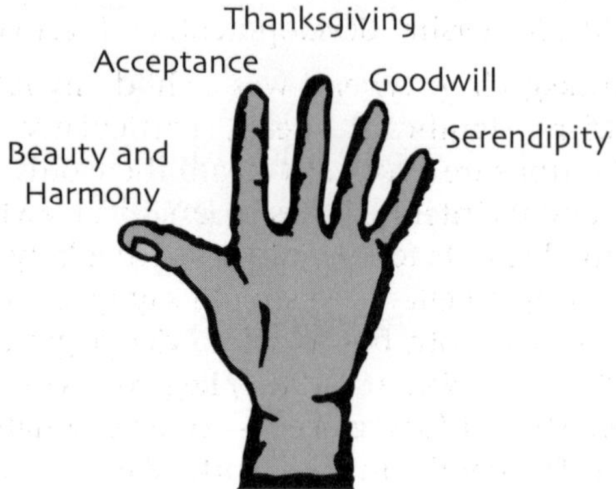

To understand and appreciate grace, we must open the hand and examine each finger independently, and understand the relationship of the fingers to one another. Each finger has its place in the world of student affairs.

Grace is beauty and harmony. Think of grace as a pleasing or attractive characteristic, quality, manner, or mode of expression. Our environments can be spaces of grace, physically and intellectually, if we design them as places for reflection, interaction, innovation, and appreciation. We are graceful in our interactions with others when we move with ease from one setting to another, equally comfortable with a concerned group of student leaders, a new president, a room filled with prospective students and their parents, or a committee of cross-divisional colleagues. Like the Graces in Greek mythology, we can be the graces of our campuses by acting as ambassadors of civility, dignity, and good manners, and by cultivating these traits in our students. As student affairs professionals we should facilitate the brilliance, joy, and potential in our people, our places, our programs, and our priorities.

Grace is acceptance. Author Joanna Macy relates, "Grace happens when we act with others on behalf of our world." We are gracious when we hold others *in good graces*, acknowledge their accomplishments, offer support in place of criticism, and act in concert with them to make a difference. We are *gracious* when we make the best of our circumstances, serve as good stewards with our resources, do the best with what we have, and accept our limitations. The practice of student affairs should include teaching students to act with others to make the world a better place through civic responsibility, leadership development, and service-learning.

Grace is thanksgiving. When I was a child, my father used to "say grace" before significant meals, particularly during the holidays, but I'm not sure I correctly heard the words of his grace. "Bless this food and its intended uses" sounded an awful lot to me like "Bless this food and its tender juices," particularly if gravy was involved. Some people believe we should say grace before meals, "not to make our food holy, but to acknowledge gratefully that it is already holy." (See McNamara, 1981.) Regardless of our religious backgrounds, we should "say grace" — or a reasonable facsimile thereof — more frequently in our work. We have much to be thankful for. We should express our thanks — to our co-workers, our colleagues, our students, and whomever or whatever inspires us — not to make our work honorable, but to acknowledge gratefully that it is already honorable.

Grace is goodwill or an act of mercy. Grace is how we honor or dignify another person. It's an interaction between the one being gracious and the one being graced, and it concerns the wills of both.

Grace involves what researcher Daniel Yankelovich (1981, 252) describes as an ethic of commitment — a shifting of the focus away from the self and toward connection with others. His ethic involves two types of commitment: closer and deeper personal relationships, and a better balance between instrumental (material) values and expressive values. In Yankelovich's examples, people give up status and high financial rewards to focus instead on enterprises that foster their self-expression and their commitment to others. "All over the country, Americans are weighing the rewards of conventional success against less lucrative but more satisfying personal achievements … ."

We should model and teach both types of commitment in our work in student affairs. To lead productive and satisfying lives, students need the capacity to develop and maintain meaningful relationships — with family members, colleagues, employers, neighbors, and significant others. They need to learn that material values can never take the place of significant emotional values: The things in life that are expressive have value in their own right, not simply in how they can be used. We need to recognize the place of goodwill in our profession; *all that we do should fall under the heading of goodwill.* Every day we're given gifts; most days, we're in the position to give our gifts to others. The giving and receiving of these gifts should be undertaken with a spirit of grace; in this way, we truly honor and dignify others and ourselves.

Grace is serendipity. "To want what I have, to take what I'm given with grace ... " (see "For My Wedding," on the Warner Bros. CD *Inside Job*, by Don Henley, 2000). Just imagine what our lives, our work, and our world would be like if we all subscribed to these words. *In The Road Less Traveled* and its sequels, author M. Scott Peck (1997) describes the synonymous nature of grace and serendipity, exclaiming that serendipity is "the gift of finding valuable or agreeable things not sought for." Although grace is available to everyone, not everyone takes advantage of it because we don't always value those things we haven't sought.

Not everyone in our profession is fond of serendipity. We can't control what we can't anticipate, and that makes us uncomfortable. "Serendipity be damned," some would say. "Let's control for all of the factors we can. Let's anticipate and prepare."

It's not that simple.

Planning and preparation are useful and desirable skills that can and should be developed. They are, to use a mathematical term, *necessary but inadequate* skills for dealing with change, uncertainty, and serendipity. Philosopher Simone Weil says, "Grace fills empty spaces, but it can only enter where there is a void to receive it, and it is grace itself which makes this void." There will always be empty spaces in our work and in our lives, and serendipity will fill these voids. How we choose to respond to the things we haven't sought is up to us. We can find serendipity and grace valuable and agreeable, or we can find them threatening. If we come to value the serendipity of grace, we have the opportunity to live life more completely. Living life more completely is not "damning serendipity." Rather, it is receiving and giving grace by promoting beauty and harmony, by practicing acceptance, by giving thanks, and by living a life of goodwill. Living life more completely involves all five fingers from the hand of grace.

In the song "Grandma's Hands," Bill Withers tells a beautiful story of his grandmother through the mannerisms and movements of her hands. Clapping in church; picking up a fallen child; issuing warnings; soothing an unwed mother; lifting a face in understanding; aching and swelling at the end of the day. The piece captures quite beautifully the hand of grace as embodied in a loving, caring, gracious, and graceful human being.

Think for a moment about your own hands. Is grace in your hands, at your fingertips?

It can be.

Listen to your life, see it for the fathomless mystery that it is.
In the boredom and pain of it no less than in the excitement and
gladness; touch, taste, smell your way to the holy and hidden
heart of it because in the last analysis all moments
are key moments, and life itself is grace.

Frederick Buechner

REFLECTION

1) What are some of the "things not sought for" in your work that you've come to find agreeable and valuable?

2) How do your spiritual or philosophical beliefs influence the way you envision grace in the workplace?

3) What is needed to make your place of work more "grace-full"?

Listen very loud to the grace within and all around you.

On Being Binked

"It's strong and it's sudden, it can be cruel sometimes,
But it might just save your life;
That's the power of love."

JOHNNY COLLA, CHRIS HAYES, AND HUEY LEWIS

I'm on a ski lift on a cold, clear February night, my face completely covered by a combination of a Vail hat, amber goggles, and the scarf knitted for me by my wife. The end of the lift appears, just over the horizon, illuminated eerily by the floodlights shining through the noisy mist generated by snow blowers. As I physically and mentally prepare to dismount, I think to myself, "It won't happen this time."

Once again, I'm wrong.

I tell my daughter to get ready. We lift the safety bar. She's on the right, I'm on the left. At just the right moment, we stand and push off from the lift. From the left side, I veer slightly to the right, following the slope that leads down from the lift. From the right side, following a form of logic I may never understand, she veers to the left. Four skis tangle and merge in a configuration never intended by the manufacturer. Skis, poles, and limbs fly off in every direction.

I've just been *binked*.

I've been binked on mountain trails, in community swimming pools, on boogie boards at the beach, and in the comfort of my own home. Actually, I've been binked many times in my life, and it's not so bad. Being binked reminds me that I'm a father; that I'm human; that things don't always go the way we think they should; that life is much larger than our expectations.

I've been binked by many people, not the least of whom is my ski companion, daughter Darci.

All of my daughters have nicknames, not of their own choosing. These nicknames weren't intentional; they just happened. They came to life, much like the personalities of the children themselves. We probably used these nicknames as much as or more than their proper names, sometimes to their mortification if their friends were present.

First-born daughter Chandra started out as Snookie Bear, but this cognomen was eventually shortened to "Snooks." The name fits her to this day, though she also answers to "CC," the name given to her by her youngest sister before she could pronounce her given name. Last-born daughter Lindsey is "Budo." I have no explanation for this name, but it also seems to fit. Darci, the middle child, is "The Bink." It is Darci's special gift that has made her nickname a verb as well as a noun.

What, you might ask, are the main ingredients in a bink? Start with an intrinsic sense of exuberance and excitability; add humor, curiosity, passion, and a little impatience; finish off the mix with a strong need to wrestle — physically, emotionally, and intellectually — with challenges, and you've got yourself a bink.

To bink or not to bink, that is the question.

To bink is to jump headlong into a situation, without full knowledge of the circumstances but with a strong belief that things will work out for the best. To bink is to experience life as it comes, with an emphasis on active participation, not passive observation. To bink is to become engaged — and sometimes entangled — in developing circumstances. To bink is to stumble, then use the obstacle as a stepping stone. To bink is to let your passion show.

As I said, being binked isn't so bad most of the time. I'm a bit of a bink myself. Some aspects of bink-ability may be hereditary, and some may be developed, but I believe it's not simply a matter of nature and nurture. No, I think there must be a universal, quantum essence that finds its way into some people and some situations. This random energy is at the very core of bink-osity. *To be binked* is to be touched — and sometimes changed — by random energy.

We who work in higher education are exposed to a wide spectrum of potential binking. Though it can come from colleagues, friends, parents, and guests, we're most likely to be binked by the students with whom we come into contact. Think about some of the students you've known who jumped headlong into situations, without full knowledge of the circumstances but with a strong belief that things would work out for the best. Think about the times you've seen students experiencing life as it comes, with active participation, not passive observation. Think about becoming engaged in the developing circumstances of a student. Think about the way some students are capable of turning any stumbling block into a stepping stone; perhaps you were the stumbling block or the stepping stone, binked in the process. Think about the students who let their passion show in their words and deeds. If my guess is correct, someone got binked — and it might have been you.

If you haven't been binked, you're not spending enough time with your students. Student affairs professionals are frequently in the direct line of fire of student enthusiasm, curiosity, experimentation, and excitement. That's where we're supposed to be.

To be binked is to be touched — and sometimes changed — by random energy.

It doesn't always feel good to be binked. Sometimes we get bruised: we misinterpret binking as a calculated assault on our ego, our body, or our spirit. When that happens, it's best to step back and gauge the intention of the *binker*. Did the student intend harm, or was it simply a matter of excessive exuberance and excitability?

Being binked should be a natural consequence of involvement in a community of higher learning. My favorite Bink just entered college. I hope she finds her college of choice to be a place where *to bink* is compatible with *to learn*. I hope she'll find faculty, staff, and friends who bink back. I hope she'll encounter student affairs professionals who help her convert her random energy into positive power. I hope she'll continue to bink a world in constant need of a little shaking up.

REFLECTION

1) Have you ever been *binked*? Describe the circumstances.

2) Do you or anyone you know have a strong need to wrestle —
   physically, emotionally, or intellectually — with challenges?
   Does this "wrestling" result in anyone being binked?

3) What actions or precautions might we take to keep from
   stifling the intrinsic exuberance, excitability, humor, curiosity,
   passion, and impatience of our students or colleagues?

   Listen very loud to the bink-ers and bink-ees in your world.

Find Your Joy

"May your hopes and dreams come true,
May you do what you can do,
Knowing only you can find your joy."

R.L. MITCHELL

Author James Cavanaugh (1990) tells a story about a group of renegades that was constantly warring with its neighboring tribes. The renegades had no morals, no love, and no compassion — very little respect for human life.

A concerned elder from one of the peaceful tribes called together leaders from all of the surrounding tribes to try to accomplish two goals: preventing the destruction brought on by the renegades, and saving the renegades from themselves. After much discussion and debate, the leaders ruled out fighting fire with fire. Rather than attempting to destroy the destroyers, they came up with an intriguing proposition: to take away the secret of joy from those who abused it, and to hide it from them forever.

But where could they hide such a significant secret? Some of the leaders suggested burying the secret deep within the earth, in the darkest, most remote cave. Others argued for hiding the secret in the ice fields of the highest mountain. Still others suggested the secret be sunk to the bottom of the sea. Each suggestion met with opposition; even the most remote hiding places were accessible and ultimately vulnerable.

Finally, the elder who called the assembly came up with the solution that all of the leaders ultimately agreed to. "Let us hide the secret of joy within the people themselves," he reasoned. "People like this will never find happiness and joy there."

To this day, some people feverishly pursue joy, searching for the secret. Relatively few ever find its hiding place: within themselves.

Joy. Rejoice. It's funny but we don't normally give much thought to joy except during the winter holidays. The rest of the year we seem to be content just being content; we're happy just being happy. The word "joy" only holds court between Thanksgiving and New Year's Day, and only then primarily as a word in a carol or on a greeting card. We seem to have forgotten what it truly means to experience joy.

A few years ago, around the holidays, I found myself juggling several questions about joy — probably in response to a Christmas song on the stereo. What is joy? Is it something that simply comes to us or must we create it? Is joy a limited resource, or is there an abundant supply that we can tap? When and where can we find joy? What does joy have to do with our vocations and avocations?

My conclusion: each of us must take responsibility for finding or creating our own joy.

Here are a few metaphors for joy. Think about how each metaphor applies to you in your work. Is joy important in the world of higher education?

Joy is a *gift*. As sentient and compassionate beings, the gift of joy comes to us through our appreciation of the stimuli we receive from a variety of sources — be they physical or metaphysical. When we're reading a book, listening to music, or viewing a painting, inspiration may be speaking to us; this is joy. When we're taking in the landscape or the changing seasons, the realization that the world is available for us to enjoy brings the amazing gift of joy to life. There are many ways the gift of joy can be a part of our work in higher education. We can illustrate and model the joy of learning, the joy of discovery, the joy of growth, the joy of new understanding, the joy of accomplishment — all of these are examples of the gifts of joy that can come about as the result of our efforts and work with students.

If joy is a gift, how good are you at giving and receiving it?

Joy is a *dance*. Born with two left feet, I'm not much of a dancer. But there are times when I'm carried away by music, by emotions, or by circumstances. Our work in higher education is also somewhat of a dance. Sometimes it's a solo we perform, dancing alone to accomplish personal or professional goals. Sometimes we harmonize in a *pas de deux*, coordinating our movements with another for mutual benefit. Sometimes we're cast in the chorus line, an important but not overly significant member of a team that is trying to make collective magic. Sometimes we're the choreographers, creating the steps and interactions for others to follow. Sometimes we're the dancers, following the directions of others. Sometimes we're the audience, taking in the wonder and spectacle of the completed dance.

If joy is a dance, how well do you know the steps?

Joy is a *journey*. The journey is not the destination; it is all of the planning that precedes the trip, all of the experiences encountered along the way, all of the learning that is accumulated, and how all of these happenings flavor the perceptions of the traveler when he or she reaches the destination. The joy we feel in reaching the destination is impacted by all of the experiences, interactions, and relationships we've encountered along the way. Along the path, we seek something beyond ourselves; we seek the supportive and joyful company of others who are seekers like we are.

Do the people you encounter in your work bring you joy? Do you bring them joy? If the answer to either question is "no," you need to determine why through reflection, self-assessment, discussion, mediation, or other interventions that might be available to you through campus or community resources. Life is far too short to be spent in joyless relationships. Our work should be filled with joy, and we should start toward that goal by being the kind of people that others look forward to working with every day.

Joy is found in *compassion*. Compassion is the ability to feel what it's like to be someone else. It's also the knowledge that there can never be peace and joy for me until there's peace and joy for you as well. Through compassion, we can find joy in the joy of others, and our joy is increased in our relationships with them. If we believe the Native American expression that tells us sorrow shared is halved and joy shared is doubled, we'd have to be crazy not to share both.

As student affairs professionals, we should be ambassadors of compassion on our campuses. We should work to make sure our campuses are progressively diverse, inclusive, and welcoming so that all students, all faculty, all staff, and all guests feel they are significant citizens within the campus community.

Joy is a *lens* through which we see. Joy is here, all around us, but we have to change our focus. If we're totally focused on budgets, blueprints, and boardrooms, we're probably not focusing on people; and if we're not focusing on people, we probably won't feel much joy. Beyond *listening* very loud, we also need to *look* very loud. Things seen through a lens of joy are always much brighter than things seen with any other lens.

What kinds of impediments get in your way and block your vision, screening the joy from your lenses?

Joy is a *choice.* When Joseph Campbell, author of *The Power of Myth* (1991), suggested that we follow our bliss, he was telling us that while we may not be able to cure the world of sorrows, we can choose to live in joy. By choosing joy, we make the world a little more joyful and a little less sorrowful.

No matter what happens to us in life, we choose how we respond. We choose every day who we are, how we're going to react to the stimuli and interactions that come before us, and what place joy will play in our emotions. We can choose to worry over the things beyond our control, or we can choose to focus on the things over which we have some degree of influence. We can choose to trust or distrust; to hope or fear; to make a mess or make amends. Some would call this free will. Whether we think the universe is based on joy or on suffering says a great deal about us, our beliefs, and our philosophies of life and work.

I believe that what I do in my work has the capacity to expand joy — in my students, in my co-workers, and in all with whom I have contact. I also understand that the potential to expand suffering exists in each of us. We get to choose. I choose to believe that the universe is based on joy — and that belief carries over into my work.

Psychologist Charlotte Davis Kasl, in her book, *Finding Joy* (1995, 189-190), writes:

> We are given a life — a precious commodity — and are placed on this earth for a short while. We are surrounded by incredible beauty, strength, and love along with incredible

violence, hatred, and prejudice. Every time a person becomes happier, they are moving one step away from prejudice and violence and closer to love and compassion. So think of your personal joy as a contribution to peace on the planet as well as food for your spirit. Filling yourself with joy takes you into a world with the "peace that passeth understanding."

Change the words "earth" and "planet" to "campus." Cast yourself in the role of a *compassionate* student affairs professional making the *choice* to see through the *lens* of joy, helping others along their *journey*, sharing the *gift* we've been given so that others can perform their own *dance* of joy.

Recently my wife and I decided to visit the local Arboretum for a springtime walk in the woods. We asked our youngest daughter if she'd like to join us. Her first response was "No, there's nothing fun there." In her way of thinking, some places are inherently fun and others aren't. Somehow, I coaxed her into joining us anyway. We enjoyed the blossoms, fed the fish, took some pictures, and, in general, had fun. Leaning over the rail of the bridge, I asked her if she was enjoying the walk; she agreed that she was. I told her, "The thing about fun is that you have to take it with you."

Joy is like that as well. You've got to take it with you. You've got to find your joy. You know where to look: it's inside of you. And inside of your colleagues. And inside of your students.

REFLECTION

1) What are some of the ways you've experienced joy in your work?

2) With whom do you share your joy?

3) What could you do to increase the amount of joy experienced in your workplace?

Listen very loud to the things that bring you joy.

Me and My Guitar

> "He never does grow impatient for
> The changes I don't know;
> If he can't go to Heaven, Lord, I don't want to go."

JAMES TAYLOR

Ever since I was a kid I knew that the Gibson Les Paul guitar was just about the best electric guitar you could buy. They age very well and they increase in value as they get older — just like musicians!

Sure, I've had other guitars in my life. My first was a Sears acoustic that I got for about $25 when I was ten. (One of my sisters eventually inherited it.) The woman I was dating during my freshman year of college gave me a nylon-string classical guitar as a gift; the guitar lasted long after the relationship went out of tune. I owned several bass guitars in high school and college — they more than paid for themselves and part of my tuition as I played in a variety of combos. I bought a used Ovation Balladeer acoustic guitar with student loan money when I was a sophomore so that I could complement the 12-string Ovation that my duo performing partner owned. He was a draft dodger from Boston who once played in the regional band Ultimate Spinach, leaving when his number came in too low and selling his electric to somebody named J. Geils. But that's another story.

When I got the first royalty check from my previous book, *Fables, Labels, and Folding Tables,* I knew what I wanted to use it for. A music store in a nearby town that specializes in guitars had a '93 Sunburst Les Paul. I talked them down a bit from their asking price and had them throw in a hard-shell case. The new guitar inspired me to get reacquainted with live music. I joined a blues band composed of aging hippies and landscapers, and I reunited with the campus-based Staff Infection, a group of faculty and staff at James Madison University that plays for campus picnics and other functions. With the gift of a multi-track recorder and a new keyboard, I also activated Studio B (as in Basement) in an unfinished room downstairs in my home. Composing and recording in my basement studio forces me to think in the logic of music. All of the music theory I learned in high school and college comes back when I have to construct a song part by part, from rhythm to vocals to instrumental leads — musical soup to nuts. I disappear into the basement for hours at a time to record. (There are much worse vices for a man to have.)

At any rate, guitars have been some of the best roommates I've ever had (short of my wife, of course). And guitars offer us some useful metaphors for the student affairs profession.

Guitars can be re-tuned when they get out of whack. A few simple adjustments and the instrument sounds great once again. Like guitars, we occasionally need to be re-tuned. For us, that may mean learning new skills, knowledges, or competencies. Even our attitudes need to be re-tuned and fine-tuned if we go askew. It would be impossible for us to always stay in tune; environmental conditions may stretch us and stress us until we're out of pitch. That's why professional development, ongoing training, and personal renewal are such important aspects of the student affairs profession.

Guitars (and pianos), unlike most other instruments, can play more than one note at a time. Subsequently, they make possible an almost endless assortment of chords and harmonies. They can be adjusted to a variety of tunings providing different moods and sounds. Like guitars, we need to be versatile. We're frequently called upon to play more than one note at a time; we have to be proficient at multitasking so that we can manage a variety of projects and responsibilities simultaneously. We need to find and create harmony with a variety of people in a variety of settings. We need to allow others to elicit unique music from us, just as we can be muses for them. We need to strike responsive chords in one another. That's why diversity, flexibility, and creativity are such important aspects of the student affairs profession.

Guitars don't mind if you make mistakes; sometimes, you learn new progressions and rhythms that way. The best thing about a long-term relationship with a musical instrument is that you learn something just about every time you pick it up. I suppose all good relationships — animate or inanimate — are the same way. Like guitars, we need to be forgiving of mistakes — the ones made by others as well as the ones we make ourselves. We should see every interaction, every project, and every assignment as an opportunity for learning and growth. We should assume that we have something to learn from everyone we encounter. That's why risk taking, lifelong learning, and tolerance are such important aspects of the student affairs profession.

Guitars don't ask for much; new strings now and then and an occasional rubdown are all they need. If you take care of them they'll take care of you. Like guitars, we probably shouldn't ask for much. The age of unlimited resources is long gone. We need to be efficient and effective, making the best possible use of what we have. A little acknowledgment, gratitude, and support go a long way toward inspiring others; so we need to dispense those precious resources liberally. That's why resourcefulness, stewardship, and recognition are such important aspects of the student affairs profession.

Guitars get better with age. The wood mellows, resulting in a deeper, richer tone. The more they're played the better they sound. They become tempered with time and use. Like guitars, we should become more valuable over time. Student affairs is a professional practice, and if practice doesn't quite make us perfect, we should at least have a deeper and richer understanding of the nuances and subtleties of our work as we become tempered with time and use. That's why modeling, mentoring, and respect are such important aspects of the student affairs profession.

When I was a young man I dreamed that music would someday make me rich. It did, but not in the way I'd assumed. As the late Harry Chapin sang many years ago, music is my life, it's not my livelihood. Student affairs is my livelihood, not my life. Music is one of the lenses I use to make meaning out of life, work, relationships, and other mysteries. I've had a relationship with the guitar for over thirty years now. I'd like to think that relationship has made me a better, more humane professional.

It isn't necessary for you to be a guitarist or any other type of musician to be a better, more humane professional. It is helpful, however, to use the avocational tools of our lives as vocational metaphors. If you're interested in photography, your camera can provide a unique lens to help you find focus in your life and work. If you're a carpentry buff, your tools can illustrate the need for diversity and variety in completing a task. If you love gardening, you can appreciate the importance of working the soil, planting the seeds, nurturing the buds, and harvesting the crop by using the right tools at the right times.

We have many instruments and tools at our disposal. The guitar is my instrument of choice. It keeps me in tune, provides my life with harmony, forgives my mistakes, doesn't ask for much, and gets better with age.

What instrument do you play?

REFLECTION

1) What are some of the ways you get re-tuned?

2) In your work, do you prefer to play one note at a time, or can you play chords and harmonies?

3) In what ways have you had to become more resourceful in work or in life in general?

Listen very loud to the instruments you use to give your life meaning.

Responsibility and Freedom: Keys To Learning

"I'm free — I'm free;
And freedom tastes of reality."

PETE TOWNSEND

Author Stephen Covey has suggested that we need a Statue of Responsibility on the West Coast to balance the Statue of Liberty on the East Coast. It's an interesting suggestion. In a land built on the precepts and principles of liberty and freedom, we have a tough time grasping the concepts and context of responsibility and obligation. Students, faculty, and staff on our campuses are quick to point out and defend their individual rights, but few are capable of articulating their accountability to the institution and its many constituents. The paradox: without responsibility, there can be no freedom. As John F. Kennedy said, "Our privileges can be no greater than our obligations. The protection of our rights can endure no longer than the performance of our responsibilities."

Like most other students before and after me, I could hardly wait for the freedom I perceived was waiting for me when I went away to college. I would be my own person; no one would be around to tell me what to do. I'd make my own rules and wear my hair the way I wanted to. I'd go to bed when I decided to and eat what I chose to. But what I didn't realize, as I packed the borrowed van to move all of my earthly belongings into a residence hall, was that the freedom I desired required that I become responsible for myself. Fortunately I had some good tutors and mentors along the

39

way. Some of them were professors; some were student affairs professionals; a few were fellow students.

Responsibility and *freedom* have been interwoven throughout history, though we find ourselves in cycles where we value one over the other. Sometimes, responsibility and freedom are on the same side of the coin; sometimes they're seen as opposites. We appear now to be in a historical cycle in which freedom takes precedence over responsibility.

Think about freedom from the perspective of a new student — free from parental control and free from the academic control imposed on them in secondary schools. Some students handle this freedom quite responsibly; others aren't quite so fortunate. "Leaving them to themselves ... [students] become the willing victims of the most totalitarian form of government ever devised — namely, submission to their peers, obeisance to people just like them. This is not freedom." These words from William Willimon, an educator and chaplain at Duke University, illustrate the potential bondage that can occur through the tyranny of peer pressure. Freedom is a good thing — a very good thing — but it can become a bad thing without responsibility.

As student affairs practitioners, we deal with issues of responsibility and freedom every day. For example, we honor and protect the constitutional freedoms of speech, assembly, and the press. We seek to develop student responsibility through leadership and service-learning programs. Unfortunately, we tend to isolate responsibility and freedom rather than cast them in the complementary roles they deserve. To be more effective in our student development capacity, we need to better understand the relationship of student responsibility and freedom to student learning and success. We need to understand the fundamental issues associated with student rights and responsibilities on the campus. This desired understanding is based on three premises:

1. **Student responsibility is the key to all development and learning** (Davis and Murrell, 1993). In their research, Davis and Murrell discovered that the habits of a person's responsible civic and personal life are refined in college. For learning to occur, students need to identify themselves with the learning process, connect to other learners, participate in a learning ethos, and engage in the life of the campus. In effect, students

must become accountable for their own learning and behavior if learning is to occur.

2. **"The freedom to learn depends upon appropriate opportunities and conditions in the classroom, on the campus, and in the larger community. Students should exercise this freedom with responsibility"** (AAHE, ACPA, and NASPA, March 1998). It's important that we distinguish between *freedom* and *liberation*; the two words have very different connotations, particularly in their relationship to student affairs work. Both of these terms are defined later in this piece; for the time being, think of freedom as being *free to do something* and liberation as being *free from external domination.*

3. **As student affairs practitioners, we have an obligation to understand the relationships among student responsibility, student freedom, and student learning** if we hope to help students take responsibility for their learning, their behavior, and their human potential in the most productive ways. We in student affairs play a significant role in helping students bridge the gap between their sometimes unpredictable behavior and our expectations for them in the learning environment.

Student Responsibility

> *"It's like there's nobody else in the world but you.*
> *In case you haven't noticed,*
> *There's lots of other people here, too."*
> Don Henley, Jai Winding, and Stan Lynch

So what's the big deal? Why should we be concerned about student responsibility? Isn't it the responsibility of the students to be responsible? Don't we "educate the best and eliminate the rest?" According to Davis and Murrell (1993, 7-8), there are four reasons for developing student responsibility in higher education:

1. **The key to student learning and student development is student responsibility.** If the student isn't responsible for his or her own learning and behavior, our efforts will be in vain. Mom and Dad can't do it, the high school counselor can't do it, and we can't do it; only the student can tap into his or her own motivation to learn. Student outcomes are tied to student effort.

2. **The academic life of the campus is diminished when students are irresponsible.** Bad apples impact the rest of the bunch; everyone suffers when anyone struggles. Irresponsible behavior in the classroom affects all members of the class, just as irresponsible behavior in the residence hall affects all members of the hall.

3. **College is where citizenship and civic responsibility are learned and refined.** If citizenship and civic responsibility aren't developed in college, they're not likely to happen after college. In every society, rights and responsibilities are articulated to its members; we have a responsibility to the society at large to fulfill our responsibility in preparing its current and future citizens.

4. **Colleges, which are in the public trust, are accountable for exercising good stewardship in the development of responsible, productive members of society.** This accountability, however, must be shared with the students themselves. It's irresponsible for a college or university to graduate and give credentials to a student who is not yet prepared to take on his or her responsibilities as a citizen.

A simple way to think of responsibility is to break the word in half — *response* and *ability* (Hersey and Blanchard, 1995; Canfield and Siccone, 1995). *Responsiveness* is defined as having the *willingness* to do something; a student who is able to perform but lacks interest or incentives needs *motivational support.* Motivational support comes through interventions intended to bolster student confidence and remove the impediments to the student's willingness and enthusiasm to engage in self-discovery. *Ability,* on the other hand, is defined as having the *skills* to do something; a student who is willing to perform but lacks competence needs *directional support.* Directional support comes through interventions intended to strengthen the student's capacity to identify, set, and attain goals.

When we think of a student having a problem with responsibility, we must consider both sides of the response-ability equation. Responsiveness relates to the "will do" of performance (motivational components), and ability relates to the "can do" of performance (cognitive ability). We might visualize these dimensions in a grid with four properties: Low Response/Low Ability,

Low Response/High Ability, Low Ability/High Response, and High Response/High Ability:

Ability

	High Response	High Response High Ability
Responsiveness	Low Ability	
	Low Response Low Ability	High Ability Low Response

Responsibility Grid

From: Canfield and Siccone. 1995.
Hersey and Blanchard. 1985.

It's critical for us as student affairs practitioners to be able to determine the difference between issues of responsiveness and issues of ability if we hope to be successful in helping students develop. Treating a responsiveness issue with an ability cure probably won't achieve the results we desire. Try this exercise:

1. Determine one or two responsibility issues on your campus. The issues could be universal (e.g., substance abuse, academic integrity) or something unique to your campus.

2. For each issue, characterize how students from each quadrant of the grid would respond to the issue. (For instance, if the issue is substance abuse, what might characterize a student's response in the low-responsiveness/high-ability quadrant?) Do this in each quadrant for each issue.

3. Next, characterize how you, as a student affairs practitioner, would intervene with students in each quadrant (motivational support, directional support, or both).

In the substance abuse scenario, a student with high responsiveness and low ability might not understand the impact that substance abuse can potentially have on academic performance and personal integrity, nor might he or she have the social skills to counter peer pressure. Nonetheless, this student might have the personal motivation to seek help or counseling; the student is willing to make a change but needs skills. Conversely, a student with low responsiveness and high ability might be well informed regarding substance abuse and social dynamics, but he or she simply doesn't care; the student knows what to do but needs a different motivation. Conceivably, there are students who could be categorized as low in responsiveness and low in ability, and thus in need of both directional and motivational support. When you identify the students who are high in responsiveness and high in ability, hire them as student peer educators!

This exercise is not designed to be used in a prescriptive manner. Rather, it's intended to demonstrate that as student affairs practitioners, we must take into account both responsiveness and ability when we're attempting to address responsibility issues on our campuses. The interventions — the things you do to address student needs related to responsibility — draw on student development and student learning theory. As always, know your capabilities and your limits. Additionally, know yourself and, when possible, know your students. Be willing to try different approaches with different students.

Student Freedom

> *"Freedom's just another word for*
> *Nothing left to lose … "*
> Kris Kristoferson

The emerging context of freedom is at the very heart of the American landscape. It's never quite been a pure context; freedom has consistently come at the cost of someone's servitude. The founders of our county who shaped a government based on freedom were, by and large, slave holders. The nation was well into its second century before the majority — women — were afforded the privileges of citizenship. The original inhabitants of the continent became less-than-second-class citizens on government reservations.

Still, the experiment of freedom continues to evolve, and people readily defend what they perceive to be threats to their freedoms. Freedom on the college campus is part of that experiment. Academic freedom is a major tenet of American higher education. The Free Speech Movement and the Civil Rights Movement in the 1960s helped to expand that freedom to students. Today, everyone on the campus seems to be well aware of his or her rights. Unfortunately, people are less attuned to their responsibilities as members of a free society. Part of the problem is that we don't fully understand what freedom means. Understanding freedom is critical in the context of student responsibility.

Isaiah Berlin (1970) has profiled the distinction between the two dominant conceptualizations of freedom in the Western tradition. Sandra Estanek (1995) has interpreted Berlin's work for student affairs practice. For the sake of our discussion, we'll refer to these concepts as *freedom* and *liberation*.

Freedom, or "positive freedom," indicates that the individual is *free to* — free to belong to the community, free to do something. This type of freedom suggests that freedom isn't doing whatever you want to do; it's doing what's appropriate. In the relationship of the individual to the community, positive freedom places the highest priority on the community. By voluntarily becoming or remaining in the community and receiving its benefits, an individual agrees to live by community values. Coming from a foundation in Greek philosophy, the basis for positive freedom is ethics and social law.

Liberation, or "negative freedom," indicates that the individual is *free from* — free from compulsion, expectation, or force. This type of freedom suggests that freedom is doing whatever you choose to do. In the relationship of the individual to the community, negative freedom places the highest priority on the individual. The individual is paramount; the community is suspect. Coming from a foundation in British and American philosophy, the basis for negative freedom is liberalism and autonomy from external determination.

We find both perspectives in American public and private higher education. An institution's mission and its defining characteristics are generally statements of positive freedom, while academic freedom is an example of negative freedom. Student development practices that stress community values and standards promote positive freedom, while laws and policies protecting certain rights and behaviors (e.g., privacy) support negative freedom. Civility and diversity efforts fall under the heading of positive freedom; the Bill of Rights champions negative freedom.

The Role of Student Affairs

> *"So concerned with matters of the heart*
> *And knowing that the millennium was just about to start*
> *And knowing that somehow we could make a difference."*
> David Crosby and James Raymond

When issues of responsibility come into conflict on the campus, it's highly likely that student affairs will be right in the middle of the controversy, and it's not uncommon for us as student affairs practitioners to be in a position to advocate for a freedom that is contradictory to the institution's position.

Estanek (1995) recommends that student affairs practitioners take a holistic view of freedom. This requires separating and analyzing both the issues and the perspectives involved (a good opportunity to listen very loud), as the student experiences the question of freedom. Student behavior and lifestyle choices may come into conflict with institutional expectations. A school may have a strong position on social issues such as abortion or gay rights; the student affairs professional may be in a position to advise a group of students who oppose the institution's policies. A student's behavior and lifestyle choices may also come into conflict with his or her own aspirations and goals. This is frequently the case in personal and career counseling interventions. Freedoms can conflict with other freedoms, just as freedoms can conflict with obligations and responsibilities.

Freedom, responsibility, and learning are interdependent abstractions that we cannot independently understand or appreciate each on their own. There can be no sustained freedom without personal responsibility and lifelong learning. There can be no meaningful learning without individual freedom and joint responsibility. There can be no practical responsibility without liberating freedom and experiential learning. As student affairs practitioners, we have an obligation to understand these relationships if we hope to help students take responsibility for their learning, behavior, and human potential.

It comes down to this: You can lead a student through college, but you can't make him or her think. You can't make them learn. You can't make them responsible, and you can't make them free. Researcher and educator C. Robert Pace (1984, 33) perhaps said it best:

> You don't have to browse in the library, you don't have to make appointments to talk with faculty members, you don't have to make outlines from your class notes, you don't have to go to concerts, you don't have to work on a committee, you don't have to ask someone to read something you've written to see if it's clear, and you don't have to have a serious discussion with students whose personal values are different than yours.

Pace believed that the most important learning comes through what he defined as *quality of effort.* Quality of effort is essentially what you don't have to do unless you're taking initiative. Quality of effort is the responsibility that one has to take in order to learn. It can only come from the student. Our job is to help students understand this principle.

REFLECTION

1) What are some examples of conflicts with positive and/or negative freedom that you or your colleagues encounter on a regular basis? How will determining the type of freedom *as it is experienced* by the student help you properly and effectively intervene?

2) How does our understanding of student responsibility and student freedom apply to our notion of "reasonable expectations" for college students?

3) If responsibility is the key to student learning, what is the lock (i.e., what primarily becomes a barrier to student learning)?

Listen very loud to your own concepts of
responsibility and freedom.

CTS Period

> "I'm tired of waiting for reason to arrive;
> It's too long we've been living these unexamined lives."

DON HENLEY

Many times in my childhood I heard my father say, "That don't make CTS period!" Children don't always understand what they hear, and it was some time before I realized that he was making a play on words. The abbreviation for "cents" is cts. — or "CTS period." It finally made sense.

As I became an adult I discovered that many things don't make CTS period. Here are just a few examples:

Neckties. If it were up to me, neck nooses would be banished as cruel and unusual punishment. I believe we'd all think a little more clearly if the circulation to our brains were restored.

High heels. A man who hated women must have created this foot fashion fetish. The untold damage to feet, legs, and backs ought to require a Surgeon General's warning.

Things that fasten behind you. Unless you're double-jointed, it's just plain unnatural to try to fasten something behind your back. Zippers, hooks, bows — Harry Houdini might have made a career out of escaping such contraptions, but the rest of us ought to be given a break.

Professional wrestling. An oxymoron if ever there was one. (Perhaps professional wrestling *is* a "sport" for oxen and morons ...). We've taken virtual violence to a new level. P.T. Barnum was right; there's a sucker born every minute, and he or she is a fan of the World Wrestling Federation.

Extra gold light beer. Once upon a time there was just beer. Someone came up with the idea of lower-calorie beer, *ergo* the introduction of light beer. Others wanted the full, rich body of European beers without the bitterness, *ergo* the introduction of extra gold beers. The marketing brew gurus then introduced extra gold light beer, which, if you're paying attention, is just plain beer. As H.L. Mencken reported, "No one ever went broke by underestimating the taste of the American public."

Enormous Sports Utility Vehicles. I'll admit it: I own an SUV — one of the smaller models. It's great in the snow and it seats five people comfortably, although most of the time it's just a commuting vehicle. In the spirit of "bigger is better," the auto manufacturers came up with larger SUVs — and even larger SUVs — and incredibly huge SUVs. They're lousy on gas mileage, they don't fit in most garages, and they cost as much as a small house, but they'll probably come out on top — literally — in a head-on collision with just about any other vehicle short of a Mack truck. Ford has the Explorer, the Expedition, and the Excursion. I have some names to suggest for their future models: the Excessive, the Extravagant, and the Exorbitant.

Panty hose. OK, I don't wear them myself, but I live in a house with my wife and three daughters. I can't imagine a less practical undergarment, and they seem to have a lifespan slightly shorter than the average housefly. Women's liberation ought to include freedom from uncomfortable, impractical unmentionables.

I could go on, but all of this is to introduce the notion that we're not immune to things that don't make CTS period in higher education.

It doesn't make CTS period when an institution encloses a Braille map of the campus in a Plexiglass case to protect it, but that happened at an institution where I used to work. On 4-feet by 8-feet sheet of quality plywood, the artist used a variety of woods to create a relief scale model of the entire campus. Each building included Braille designations for entrances, handicap ramps, and building names. For the sighted the map was a work of art and beauty. For the visually impaired the map was a useful tool for navigating the campus. But the director of disability services, concerned that the map might be damaged, had it enclosed.

It doesn't make CTS period when an institution installs a touch-tone registration system for the campus, only to discover that the campus is still using a rotary phone system. Strange, but true.

It doesn't make CTS period when institutions locate integral student services in remote parts of the campus. Prior to our student success efforts at my current institution (James Madison University), Registration Services, Student Accounting, and Financial Aid couldn't have been farther apart, literally and figuratively. Our students referred to this setup as the Bermuda Triangle; somewhere between these distant offices, things got confused or lost. Other students remarked that the arrangement was like traveling through Europe; each office was like a separate country, with different borders, languages, customs, and currencies. Breaking down these artificial boundaries became a primary objective in our effort to make a little CTS period out of the mess we'd created.

It doesn't make CTS period when we help students develop their leadership capacity, then express our dismay when they use that capacity to challenge our policies and procedures.

It doesn't make CTS period when we let parents assume full responsibility for their students' problems and concerns — at the expense of the student's development of personal responsibility.

It doesn't make CTS period when we forget that the primary reason students are on our campuses is to learn. If we're spending time, money, or other assets on programs or services that don't have measurable learning and development outcomes tied to the institutional mission, we're misusing our resources.

It doesn't make CTS period when we think and act departmentally rather than universally. We are a part of the whole, not apart from the whole. Our goals and objectives should be derived from the institution's mission, not *vice versa*. It's not enough to perform our functions well; we also need to interact and intersect effectively with the rest of the campus community.

To make CTS period, we need to be sensible and sensitive. We need to be perceptive and reasonable, show good judgment, and make good use of our critical thinking skills. We need to be open to and aware of the needs and expectations of others. In effect, we need to come to our senses if we hope to make sense of our world for ourselves and for our students. Anything less would be senseless.

I have trouble with the term "common sense." Common sense is all too frequently the mantra of people who are afraid of education or educated people. What we need is *uncommon* sense; new ways of looking at things. We need to break free of "conventional" wisdom. *Unconventional* wisdom may provide us with solutions to the age-old problems like prejudice, injustice, and aggression — conditions that haven't been rectified by conventional means.

Socrates wondered if the unexamined life was worth living. We have a unique opportunity in our profession to model and teach life-examination skills by giving our students the gifts of reflection and critical thinking. Perhaps they'll be able to create changes and challenge our institutions to make CTS period out of the illogical things we sometimes do.

REFLECTION

1) What are some of the things in your professional experience that just don't make CTS period?

2) How do you model sensibility and sensitivity in your work? Who are your models in these regards?

3) Does your campus have any "Bermuda Triangles"? What can you do to eliminate them?

   Listen very loud to the things that make CTS period to you, your colleagues, and the students you work with.

Shooting for the Stars

ALLAN TOUSSAINT

Jiminy Cricket assured us when we were young that dreams could come true if we wished on a particular star. We've all learned through experience and maturity that it takes a little more than simply wishing if our dreams are to be realized. But a dream is still a good place to start.

What is *success*? Is it something you get? Something you own? Something you are? Something you do? All of the above? None of the above?

Education should prepare people for a life of success, but that might be a tenuous target if we can't decide what success means.

When I was asked to develop a student success focus for our campus, I engaged in numerous discussions about the nature of success. I asked faculty, staff, colleagues from other campuses, and a wide range of students about what success meant to them. For some, it meant retention: keeping students in school so they could make progress toward a terminal degree. For others, student success meant remediation: providing academic support for students who struggle with the learning process. For others still, student success meant freshman year programs designed to help students successfully navigate the college experience. In some cases, student success simply meant doing a better job of providing academic advising.

Student success can mean all of these things and more, but I wanted to find some common threads that would help frame success in universal, meaningful ways. I wished to develop memorable images that would capture the essence of success and be useful in an array of applications. From the many discussions, focus groups, and informal conversations I'd had, I envisioned a five-point star reflecting the five qualities of success:

1. The *dream* of success ... having a *vision.*
2. The *road* to success ... having a *plan.*
3. The *challenge* of success ... having *determination.*
4. The *secret* of success ... having *passion.*
5. The *pursuit* of success ... having *motivation.*

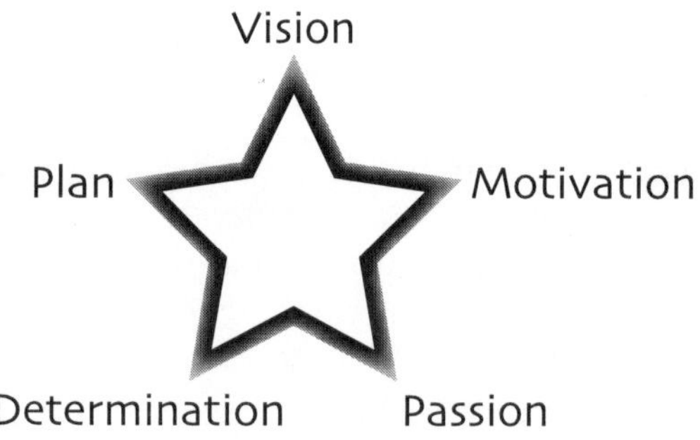

The *dream* of success ... having a *vision.* The key to happiness is having dreams; the key to success is making dreams come true; the key to making dreams come true is inspiration; the key to inspiration is having a vision. Dr. Martin Luther King, Jr., had such a vision and, though it cost him his life, his vision carried him and millions more to the very "mountaintops" he described.

Visions don't relate to material possessions; they correspond with sacred, expressive values. Having a home is a vision; having a larger house isn't. Getting an education is a vision; getting a degree isn't. Living a satisfying, meaningful life is a vision; making a boatload of money isn't.

The problem with most of our visions is that we tend to shoot too low. Several years ago, I participated as a facilitator in a national leadership seminar with a group of student leaders from across the country. One of the tasks we had for the students was to identify the vision for their respective organizations. One student, the president of a fraternity, said it was his vision to get more members to join the group. I asked him why; he said the fraternity needed more members or the organization would collapse. I challenged him: "Why would I want to join an organization whose primary purpose is to attract more members so the group won't fold? What is the real purpose of the organization?" He said it was to foster brotherhood and provide public service. I asked him why that was important; he said, "So we can make the world a better place." I replied, "Now, you're getting closer to a vision for your organization." Getting more members wasn't the goal: the goal was to inspire others to join a group with a significant purpose. He and his group needed to shoot much higher. They needed to start with a dream, a vision of success.

The *road* to success ... having a *plan*. You've probably seen the posters, notepads, and T-shirts that say, "Success is a journey, not a destination." My campus has adopted the phrase, "The road to student success," with a logo illustrating a winding road culminating in a sunset. Success isn't where you end up; it's how you get there. And how you get there has a lot to do with having a plan. As professional golfing legend Arnold Palmer puts it, "The road to success is always under construction." Each student we work with is ultimately responsible for charting a course and navigating his or her own way through the unexpected circumstances of life. Planning can't be unconditional; flexibility is essential, because you never know where the road is going to take you.

Of all the things we should be teaching our students, planning should be at the top of the list. I've identified some planning fundamentals that must be observed if our plans are to have their greatest potential for success (Mitchell, 1987). You might look at these fundamentals as the "7 Rules of the Road for Planning the Road to Success":

1. A plan is a detailed scheme for *accomplishing an objective* (what).

2. Plans are *time-dependent* (when).

3. A plan must be *written/recorded* and be accessible or visible (where).

4. A plan depends on clear *communication* in order to be activated (how).

5. Plans must give full *consideration* to the people affected by or affecting the plan (who).

6. Plans must be *flexible, simple,* and *relevant* (why).

7. Plans must include *alternatives* (what if).

The *challenge* of success ... having *determination*. I've never yet, in my forty-five-plus years, taken a journey during which something unexpected didn't happen. The journey could be literal or figurative; it doesn't matter. Sometimes it's my fault, sometimes it's not, but that's irrelevant. Obstacles happen. Author James E. Gibson tells us, "The absence of obstacles is never the reason for success. True success lies in learning to overcome them."

I've thought a great deal about Gibson's comment and how it relates to our work in student affairs. I'm not sure we're doing enough to teach our students how to overcome obstacles. On our campuses, we go out of our way to *remove* obstacles — as we should — to their learning and development. Yet obstacles will happen, no matter how good we are at anticipating and removing them. How can we both remove obstacles and help students develop the skills and knowledge they'll need to *surmount* them throughout their lives?

Let's start by modeling and teaching *determination* to our students, distinguished here from *inflexibility.* Determination is defined as problem solving and conscious decision making based on purpose and belief; it involves persistence, conviction, and resolution. Inflexibility is defined as the closed-minded exertion of one's will and a resistance to change of any kind; it involves rigidity, stubbornness, and obstinacy. The lesson students must learn — through general education curricula, active and experiential learning activities, and student development interventions (e.g., cultural awareness, civic responsibility, teamwork) — is how to develop and manage personal determination based on purpose without resorting to inflexibility based on ignorance. A student's determination leads to success; a student's inflexibility leads to failure. With determination, students can convert obstacles into stepping-stones; with inflexibility, obstacles become roadblocks.

We in student affairs can and should play a significant role in helping students distinguish the difference between determination and inflexibility. Determination can be an outcome of our leadership development programs, our outdoor education seminars, or our collaborative efforts with appropriate general education classes. Lists of feature films depicting themes of determination (e.g., "Hope Floats," "28 Days," "Hurricane Streets") are available from a variety of web site databases. (One excellent site is at www.spiritualityhealth.com. It includes a searchable database of books, videotapes, and audiotapes on a variety of subjects). Determination can also be a reflection subject for service-learning projects.

With determination, you as a student affairs professional can come up with additional ideas on how you can teach and model determination.

The *secret* of success ... having *passion*. Over the years, many secrets to success have been touted. Some people have pushed get-rich-quick or pyramid schemes that only benefited the originators. Others have filled books with aphorisms and maxims on success; interesting thoughts to ponder, but they don't translate into meaningful applications for our students or for us.

I believe there *is* a secret, and that the secret's out: it's *passion*. Not the passion found in steamy videos; not the passion that leads to road rage and other crimes. It's the passion that's based on boundless enthusiasm and love. Will Rogers, the legendary American humorist who probably never met a student affairs professional he didn't like, said: "If you want to be successful, it's just this simple. Know what you're doing. Love what you're doing. And believe in what you're doing." It's not likely that anyone will ever be truly successful at something he or she absolutely loathes.

Think for a moment of some of the most dynamic speakers you've ever listened to; some of the best concerts you've ever heard; some of the best films or plays you've seen; some of the most exciting athletic contests you've attended; your own life. What would happen if these performances were without passion? We've only got one opportunity to live this life. Regardless of our personal circumstances, we can choose to live life with or without passion. I believe that passion — for life, for our relationships, and for the work we've chosen to do — is a critical factor in our happiness and success. I also believe that we can model this passion for life, relationships, and work for our students, so that their lives can be more productive and meaningful. Passion is an abundant resource that can never expire. We can waste it, however, if we keep it dormant.

Is there a place for passion in the student affairs profession? Philosopher Sivanda Sarasvati said, "Put your heart, mind, intellect, and soul even to the smallest acts. This is the secret of success." We should put our hearts, minds, intellects, and souls into "even the smallest acts" we do too.

The *pursuit* of success ... having *motivation*. Beyond having a vision, a plan, determination, and passion, we need motivation to actually bring success to life. I once heard motivation described this way: A car, fully equipped, maintained, and fueled, *has the potential to go*. What it lacks is the capacity to know when to go, or where to go, or how to go, or why to go, or what to take. What it lacks is *motivation*. Motivation is the human element that realizes the capacity of the car to go. Motivation is the force that steers the car, not just physically but philosophically as well. Even in the age of computers, motivation is still a *human* factor — and perhaps the most important aspect of human motivation is the capacity to ask questions.

Why I am going to college? What am I going to do with my life? How will I know if a major or career is right for me? Is college worth the time, money, and energy that I'll have to invest? Will college help me discover who I am? The answers to these and other questions become the motivations for an individual student's success. And although we can provide support and resources, the student ultimately must answer the questions. Not the advisor. Not the roommate. Not the parents. The student.

Earlier, I mentioned some of the many motivations campuses have for developing a student success focus. As we studied the question of student success at James Madison University, where I currently work, we came up with three primary motivations:

1. To help students make successful transitions into, through, and out of the university.

2. To encourage student responsibility and motivation for learning and behavior.
3. To support students with cohesive services based on common educational objectives.

Having worked with this model for nearly five years now, I've come to recognize an overlap between our student success model (successful transition, motivation to learn, and cohesive service) and the five qualities of success described above (vision, plan, determination, passion, and motivation). It goes like this:

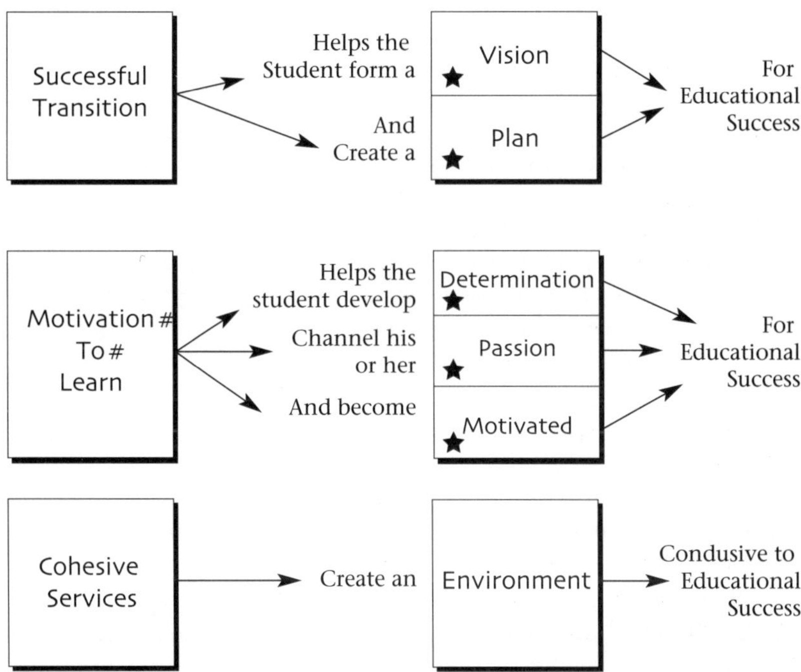

Reading from left to right:

1. Successful transition (into, through, and out of the institution) helps the student form a vision and create a plan that will lead to educational success. For this reason, we in student affairs should develop programs and services (e.g.,

orientation, residence life activities, career planning) to help students make successful transitions.

2. The student's motivation to learn helps him or her develop determination, appropriately channel his or her passion, and become motivated to achieve educational success. For this reason, we in student affairs should develop programs and services (e.g., Freshman Year Experience, leadership activities, service-learning) to help students develop self-responsibility and motivation to learn.

3. Finally, we in student affairs have a responsibility to make programs and services cohesive, accessible, and welcoming (e.g., student success centers, "one-stop shopping," web-based resources); this approach creates an environment that is most conducive to students' educational success.

In effect, our primary motivation as an institution is to prepare "students to be enlightened and educated citizens who will lead productive and meaningful lives" (James Madison University's mission). We accomplish this mission by articulating and developing the philosophy of students' responsibility for their own motivation to learn. Students are successful when they assume this responsibility.

What is success? Writer Henry David Thoreau captured the combination of vision, planning, determination, passion, and motivation in one sentence: "If one advances confidently in the direction of his dreams, and endeavors to live the life which he has imagined, he will meet with a success unexpected in common hours."

To briefly review: success is a star with five points. It's having a dream or vision and knowing what inspiration will help you reach the dream. It's having a plan and knowing what direction you're heading. It's having determination, realizing the place of obstacles, and facing the challenges. It's having the not-so-secret passion of boundless enthusiasm and love for what you do. It's having the motivation to pursue the vision, create the plan, foster the determination, and follow the passion wherever it leads.

Success is too important to be measured only in terms of money and recognition. If your definition of success focuses primarily on fame and fortune, this may not be the book for you — and student affairs is definitely not the career for you. Fame and fortune may result indirectly from a successful college experience. But these objectives have far less value than the *true objective of higher education:* to give students the knowledge, skills, and competencies they will need to navigate the rest of their lives.

Wishing on a star isn't enough. We must teach our students and colleagues to create their visions, plan their trips, and use their determination, passion, and motivation to discover the stars — whether those stars are light years away or in one's own back yard.

REFLECTION

1) What are some potential visioning and planning exercises that could be useful in helping students through their transitions into, through, and out of your institution?

2) How might a student's developmental maturity affect his or her capacity to distinguish between determination and inflexibility?

3) What can you do to create more cohesive services and a more supportive campus environment for students?

Listen very loud to your perceptions of success,
and shoot for the stars.

A Learning Community in the Real World

"Your weekend at the college didn't
turn out like you planned;
The things they passed for knowledge,
I can't understand."

More than ever before, the decision about which college to attend is filled with almost unlimited choices. The *2000 Higher Education Directory* lists 2,322 private and 1,649 public institutions of higher education currently operating in the United States; that's 3,971 campuses! It's getting much harder for students to answer for themselves, "Which is the right one?"

We in student affairs (and, indeed, in all of higher education) should communicate more effectively to all of our potential students and their families that selecting a college is selecting a *community*. There are many options, and some options are more fitting than others.

Why a community? Porter Butts, the "father" of the student union movement, offered this insight many years ago: "I sometimes think too much emphasis is placed on college as a preparation for life. We overlook that college is life — four precious years of it." College, in fact, is "the real world" for hundreds of thousands of people every year. I can't imagine looking at any other two- to four-year period in our adult lives and imagining that it's

just a dress rehearsal for better things to come. College is life —
and we in student affairs can play an important role in helping
students make informed choices so that later on, they won't feel
those years were wasted.

Let's begin thinking — and promoting the idea — of college as
a learning community, not simply the next level in a student's
education. College is not higher high school, and students aren't
majoring in "Pre-Life." For two, four, six years or more, college
becomes the life and the world of the full-time student, day and
night, barring the occasional holiday visit or summer break that
takes the student to his or her other home. Even the part-time
student spends a significant percentage of his or her time on the
campus.

A learning community is much more than a campus; it
becomes the primary community for students. It's where they
spend a large proportion of their waking hours (and the rest of
their hours if they're residential …). It's where they find their
friends and, for some, their partners. It's where they study, eat,
play, work, think, and grow. Like the best communities, colleges
care about each individual person, offering programs, services,
support, and challenges to make his or her experience meaningful
and productive. Like all communities, colleges have issues that
members must work together to resolve.

It's within the learning community that students develop the
capacity to become citizens and contributing members of society.
It's here that students potentially develop their individuality apart
from family. It's here that they have the opportunity to determine
their purpose in life.

The learning community has an incredible impact on whether
or not a student develops. That's why an informed choice and a
good fit are so important. We can't imagine anyone spending
time and money buying clothes that don't fit. It's hard to fathom
spending far more time and money selecting a college that
doesn't fit, but some students spend less time selecting a college
than they do a wardrobe. And just as you probably wouldn't be
comfortable wearing *your* parent's old clothes — the size or the
style may not suit your shape or tastes — there's a good chance
that your child won't be comfortable wearing *your* old college.
One size does *not* fit all.

When the college doesn't fit, the student still has choices. He or she may be able to adapt and try to improve the fit. The lack of fit may be due to environmental factors, developmental factors, or adjustment factors. Most campuses provide services to help students make these kinds of modifications.

The student may also realize that there are other factors in his or her personal or social life that need attention — that the campus fit is really symptomatic of other personal considerations. Again, counseling may help the student identify potential alternatives. In the final analysis, identifying a new community with a better fit may be what the student wants or needs. Moving on can be a good thing, if it increases the student's chances of realizing his or her goals.

The learning community is also where we work. As student affairs professionals, we spend a fair percentage of our waking hours there as well! It's where many of us find our friends and partners. It's where we continue to study, eat, play, work, think, and grow. Our college communities often offer us assistance programs and services with support and challenges to make our experiences meaningful and productive. As in all communities, we find ourselves in (and we sometimes cause) the issues and problems requiring community solutions. It's within this learning community that we practice our citizenship and individuality and try to make meaningful contributions. It's here that we have the opportunity to accomplish our purpose in life.

The learning community we select as our place of work has an incredible impact on whether or not we continue to develop. That's why an informed choice and a good fit are so important. One size does *not* fit all: "Which is the right one for me?"

When the college doesn't fit, we too still have choices. The grass isn't always greener on another campus; sometimes we need to adapt and try to improve the fit. As is sometimes the case with students, our lack of fit may be due to environmental factors, developmental factors, or adjustment factors. We may also realize that there are other factors in our personal or social life that need attention. Career counseling — it's never too late — may help us identify potential alternatives. In the final analysis, identifying a new community with a better fit may be what we want or need. Moving on can be a good thing, if it increases our chances of realizing our goals. Moving on is less of a good thing if the baggage we take with us is our real burden.

The Carnegie Foundation for the Advancement of Teaching (1990) has identified six principles that should define the kind of community every higher education institution should strive to be:

1. An *educationally purposeful* community (collaborative learning)
2. An *open* community (freedom and civility)
3. A *just* community (individuality and diversity)
4. A *disciplined* community (responsibility and common good)
5. A *caring* community (support and service)
6. A *celebrative* community (heritage and affirmation)

To make our campuses true learning communities, we need to address several questions related to these principles. Student affairs should play a leadership role in bringing these questions to the collective consciousness of the community. Questions based on each of these principles are included below in an expanded "Reflection" section. How your institution asks, discusses, and answers these questions may tell you a great deal about the type of learning community it aspires to be and whether you might have a good fit with the community.

(**Suggestion for graduate students:** Use some of these questions in your professional position interviews when someone invariably asks you, "Do you have any questions for us?")

For many of us in student affairs, college was life — four (or more) precious years of it — followed by a lifetime of satisfying and challenging work. I hope I never "grow up" and leave college; it's my learning community in the real world.

REFLECTION

1) How educationally purposeful is our campus? Are all programs, services, and activities based on educational objectives? Is collaboration expected or merely encouraged? Do students understand the connections among various classes and between their curricular and co-curricular programs? Do we have an ethos of excellence and scholarship, or one of activity and stimulation? Are we an educationally purposeful community?

2) How open is our campus? Do all people experience a sense of freedom here, or is freedom based on power? Is civility the rule of thumb, or is it a rule to be enforced? Is freedom a special privilege for some community members and not for others (e.g., academic freedom for faculty but not others)? Are people free to do whatever they want, or are there boundaries to freedom? Are we an open community? ("A Learning Community in the Real World")

3) How just is our campus? What role does fairness play in assignments, grading, and decision making? Does justice mean treating everyone the same? Is justice more important than compassion? Does the majority always rule? What consideration is given to individual differences and needs? Are we a just community?

4) How disciplined is our campus? When do community interests and the common good take precedence over individual interests? Do all members of the community understand their civic responsibilities to the rest of the community? Are campus expectations reasonable and appropriate? What does it mean to be a good citizen? How does the campus handle disturbances and inappropriate behavior? Are we a disciplined community?

5) How caring is our campus? How do we respond to individual and group crises? Does our campus have any physical, psychological, social, or economic barriers that make it impossible for some people to succeed here? Do student needs drive budgets, or is it vice versa? Do the people who work here like each other? How do we handle staff concerns? Are we a caring community?

6) How celebrative is our campus? What traditions, rituals, ceremonies, and practices define us as a community? How do we celebrate the transitions of all members of our community into, through, and out of the institution? What do we honor and why? How do we celebrate diversity and unity simultaneously? Who are our heroes and heroines? What are our symbols? Are we a celebrative community?

Listen very loud to the ways you contribute to and benefit from a sense of community.

Motivation Revisited or (Mr. Peabody's "Wayback Time Machine")

> "I wanna go back and do it all over
> But I can't go back, I know."
>
> EDDIE MONEY

Motivation is an interesting, albeit frequently misunderstood, word. The question, "What can I do to motivate my students?" has only one answer: nothing. It's impossible for any one of us to motivate anyone else; we can only motivate ourselves. The root word of motivation is *motive:* an impulse acting as a stimulus to action. We can't give anyone else a motive or an impulse; the motive or impulse must come from within.

But we *can* create an environment and conditions in which the other individual's motivation comes to life. Our primary responsibility as student affairs professionals is to *create the kind of environment and the conditions in which our students' motivation about learning, meaningful work, and purpose in life result in their impulse to take action.* To meet this responsibility, we need to understand our own motivations and how they may differ from those of our students. Without this understanding, we're going to be frustrated in our relationships with students.

It's common knowledge that people want to do the things they find rewarding and avoid the things they don't find rewarding. Researchers have found that a college student's motivation is influenced by two factors:

1. What the student perceives as important, and
2. What the student believes he or she can accomplish.

"Students are more likely to be motivated if their needs are being met, if they see value in what they are learning, and if they believe that they are able to succeed with reasonable effort," write McMillan and Forsythe (1991).

So how do we create an environment that will help our students decide what is truly important in their lives and in their future work? How can we help them believe in themselves and their potential? What role can we play in helping them choose appropriate higher education paths? What conditions do we need to create? We must start by learning about students' *motivations*.

Like most student affairs professionals, you want your students to be successful in college; that's *your* motivation. My motivation is to give you some skills, tools, insights, and suggestions — in effect, to create an environment and conditions in which your motivation can be supported — because I believe the student affairs profession is uniquely equipped to help students succeed. It's up to you how you will use these resources to create the environment and conditions to support your students' motivation.

Let's look at student motivation through the following four questions:

1. Why do students want to go to college?
2. What do students hope to accomplish in college?
3. What skills/knowledge/competencies do students have, and which ones will they need to be successful?
4. How much are students willing to invest?

Why do students wants to go to college?

Before answering this question, you need to get acquainted with Mr. Peabody's "Wayback Time Machine," hereafter referred to as the *MPW*. Remember Mr. Peabody? He was the little cartoon dog on the old "Rocky and Bullwinkle" show who traveled back in time to teach Sherman, his faithful human servant, important lessons in history. I'll be using the *MPW* device periodically throughout this essay; whenever you see the acronym *MPW* or hear the sound of the machine working *(Zzzziiiippppp!)*, you'll know it's time to travel to your own past or back again. So, here's your first *MPW* …

Zzzziiiipppp! You're now eighteen years old again. The music of the day is on your radio. Old, familiar faces appear on your television. Hair and clothing styles that seem so silly to today's youth are once again in fashion. How does your world look and feel? Are you thinking about going to college? Are you pursuing other options, like work, starting a family, or going into the military? Who are you and what do you hope to accomplish? What decisions do you have to make, and what decisions will be made for you? What are your hopes and dreams, your fears and concerns? What are your parents' expectations for you and how do their expectations differ from your own?

Keep in mind this picture of the world as you knew it at age eighteen. The *MPW* is now taking you back to the present.

Zzzziiiippppp! Has the world changed? What influences that weren't necessarily a part of your upbringing have helped to shape the lives of today's students? What do we know now as a society that we didn't know then? The distinctions between your world at eighteen and the world of today's students is going to be a critical consideration as you look at their motivation to attend college.

With these distinctions in mind, why do you think today's student wants to go to college, generally speaking? To become wise? To get rich? To find a mate? To discover his or her destiny? All of the above? None of the above? Rather than simply assuming you know why your students have chosen to go to college, why not ask them? To effectively help your student in all that follows them, you need to be able to:

1. Identify the reasons why today's students choose to go to college.
2. Identify the reasons why you chose to go to college.
3. Honor the differences in your respective motivations.
4. Explore how you can help today's students clarify their expectations of the college experience.

Addressing these tasks will help you begin to focus on the possibility of success for particular students. If your students can actually see themselves comfortably navigating the college campus — attending classes, using the library and the Internet for study, getting involved in student life — then, and only then, can they begin to imagine being successful in that enterprise. As a student affairs professional, you create the environment in which they can engage in this "imagineering" activity without fear of criticism or correction. That's why it's so important to separate your own motivations from those of your students.

What do students hope to accomplish in college?

Let's climb back into the *MPW. Zzzziiipppp!* We're back in the world of your youth. If you chose to attend college, you probably realized early on that *going to college* was something quite different from getting something out of college, and that *getting something out of college* had a direct correlation with *putting something into college.*

Going to college could be a fairly passive experience. As one college professor recently remarked about his institution, "You can get a good education here, but it's not required." College is an incredible banquet, but no one forces you to have a balanced meal. You might have discovered in your youth that there were shortcuts to learning. Some shortcuts — published study notes and guides — were socially acceptable, although serious professors probably frowned upon them. Other shortcuts can only be called what they really are: cheating. Most of us hope that our doctors, dentists, and air traffic controllers didn't cheat or take any short-cuts in their education. It's hard to imagine any profession in which it would be desirable for the practitioners to receive their credentials without the full benefit of the skills, knowledge, and competency achieved through study, hard work, and application. Going to college isn't enough; getting something out of college requires putting something into college.

Zzzziiipppp! The *MPW* has brought us back to the present. Because of the relationships involved in our work, many of us student affairs professionals have the opportunity to get to know students better than anyone else on campus does. What do you think your students hope to accomplish in college? Your role here is to help your students distinguish the differences among:

1. Why I *want to go* to college,
2. What I *hope to get out* of college, and
3. What I'll *need to put into* college.

You can provide parameters for students to consider. Use the following three "lenses," which can be universally related to the motivation to attend college — to search for knowledge, to search for a career, and to search for a life:

Knowledge. In discussion with your students, ask:

1. What types of things will you *know about* (knowledge) after graduation that you don't know about now?
2. What types of things will you *be able to do* (skills) after graduation that you can't do now?
3. How do you imagine you will be different as a result of the college experience?

Career. In discussion with your students, ask:

4. Who are some of the people you admire in their work?
5. If you had the choice to do any conceivable job (the sky's the limit), what would it be?
6. What role will work play in your life, and how will college help you prepare for the world of work?

Life. In discussion with your students, ask:

7. What are some of the most important tangible things you hope to accomplish in your life (e.g., financial security, property)?
8. What are some of the most important non-tangible things you hope to accomplish in your life (e.g., success, happiness)?
9. How will college prepare you for the type of life you'd like to lead?

It won't work to impose your own values on these prospective students. Your hopes and dreams don't count here. Don't saddle your students with your expectations; help them develop their own.

What skills/knowledge/competencies do students have, and which ones will they need to be successful?

If students have successfully navigated elementary and secondary school, there's a good chance they have skills, knowledge, and competencies in a number of areas. Unfortunately we in higher education don't do a very good job of helping students inventory these traits. Wouldn't it be great if every student about to enter college had a personal transcript that went beyond class listings and positions held, focusing instead on *what he or she knows* and *what he or she can do?* Some students may be blessed with just such a document; all others may have difficulty recounting where they've been and what they've accomplished.

Zzzziiiipppp! Stepping out of the *MPW*, you discover that you're once again graduating from high school; the commencement speaker has used up all of the usual clichés about your generation being the future. It's hard for you to think about the future because your mind is overflowing with images from your past. This thing called high school is over forever; it all went by so quickly.

At this critical moment in your high school career, do you have any idea of *who you are, what you know*, and *what you can do?* Probably not. Nonetheless, you have to make sense of these thoughts over the coming summer months, whether or not you're headed for college.

Zzzziiiipppp! Fast-forward to the present. Our soon-to-be college freshmen are graduating from high school, still hearing the same commencement clichés with a few contemporary references thrown in. As these students pick up their diplomas, do you think they have a sense of *who they are, what they know*, and *what they can do?* Probably not. We get our chance to help them take stock.

Educator Russell Edgerton once said: "Students learn *about things* by listening. They learn *how to do things* by doing them. They learn understanding and judgment through immersion and intense encounters, being in the play rather than just reading it" (emphasis mine). Being "in the play" and being active learners requires skills, knowledge, and competency.

Skill (how to do it) refers to proficiency, ability, or technique that generally requires use of the hands, the body, or the mind. Skill must be acquired and developed, and it relates to behavior needed in specific situations. *Having skill* means having the capacity to perform certain actions or functions. Skills are generally associated with dexterity and aptitude in tasks like writing, listening, speaking, drawing, swimming, and calculating.

Unfortunately, without *knowledge*, skills have limited applicability. Knowing how to do something without knowing why, when, where, or with whom can be dangerous.

Knowledge (that which is known) refers to familiarity with, awareness of, and understanding of information, generally gained through experience or study. Knowledge relates to the acquisition of, the retention of, and the capacity to recall content, information, and experience. *Having knowledge* means having the capacity to apply knowledge in appropriate ways. Knowledge is generally associated with cognitive disciplines like grammar, history, and science.

Unfortunately, without competency, knowledge has limited applicability. Knowing what is known without being able to do anything with that knowledge can be frustrating.

Competency (knowing, being, and doing) refers to the ability to cluster related knowledge, attitudes, and skills. Competency is about performance that can be measured and improved. Where skills are situational and specific, competencies are generic and universal. *Being competent* implies having skills, knowledge, and the correct attitude to perform appropriately. Competencies are generally associated with performance tasks on the job, like identifying and solving problems, weighing risks and making decisions, planning and scheduling work, and setting goals and standards. Competency results in productive performance.

Ask your students the following questions. Have them list their responses for each. (Note: This can also be a valuable personal reflection exercise; it's a great foundation for creating a personal and/or professional development plan.)

1. **Skills.** What are your skills? What do you know how to do? In what skills do you wish you were stronger? Are there skills you'll need in college that you currently don't have?

2. **Knowledge.** What do you know? In which topics or areas of content do you have a strong sense of understanding or mastery? In which areas of knowledge do you wish you were stronger? Is there knowledge you'll need in college that you currently don't have?

3. **Competency.** What are your competencies? In what ways are you competent? In what competencies do you wish you were stronger? Are there competencies you'll need in college that you currently don't have?

Students and their advisors can continuously refer to these lists to gauge progress and see what remains to be done.

How much are students willing to invest?

Zzzziiiipppp! You're finally headed for college. How in the world are you going to pay for it? Student loans? Scholarships? Student employment? Your parents or other supporters might be backing your education, but you're probably going to have to take responsibility for some of the expenses. Perhaps you're totally responsible for paying for your education. Is it going to be worth it?

Zzzziiiipppp! I tell parents in college orientation presentations that college is expensive. The only thing more expensive than a college education is the lack of one. Higher education isn't cheap. It's one of the most expensive things you can do with your money. In simple terms, college costs more than most new cars and less than most new houses. In more complex terms, *there are no simple terms* related to the cost and value of a college degree. It's important to get the proper perspective on the cost of college before we can go much further.

First and foremost, a college education can't be purchased. Learning can't be consumed; it can only be produced through the active involvement of the learner. A student (or a student's parents) can't buy college; they pay tuition and fees for the opportunity to learn.

Second, college is an investment. The return on this investment is realized over a lifetime, not simply in the first job after college. A lifetime of work, a lifetime of learning, and a lifetime of *life* are the payoff.

Third, the investment of money is only one part of the equation. College takes time. For every hour spent in the classroom, two to three hours of study should be spent outside the classroom. Group projects, library research, lab work — college represents a significant commitment of time. College also takes energy — mental energy, emotional energy, physical energy, even spiritual energy. College requires concentration, focus, and a passion for learning; invest anything less and you're wasting your time.

So if learning must be produced rather than consumed, and if college is an investment, and if college takes time and energy, how much is a college education worth to your students? They could easily spend their money, time, and energy on a world of other things. Perhaps a more thought-provoking question: "What's the cost of *not* attending college?" What will a student lose in terms of competitiveness in the workplace; depth of understanding of the world where he or she lives; depth of self-assessment; access to ideas and emerging technologies; development of citizenship and responsibility; development of the capacity to think, integrate, and synthesize ideas and effectively use resources?

Part of the decision to attend college should be a costs/benefits analysis. Do this with your students: have them mark a piece of paper with two columns, one labeled "Costs" and the other "Benefits." Under "Costs," have your students write down all they're giving up to attend college (e.g., time, money, high school friendships). Under "Benefits," have your students write down all they'll receive by attending college (e.g., new skills, knowledge, career opportunities).

Costs	Benefits

Which list is longer? Which list is focused on the present, and which is focused on the future? Which list is based on hope and possibility?

The point of this exercise is for students to realize that anything worthwhile comes with an investment. College is only "worth it" if a student is willing to pay the cost in time, energy, and money. College is only "worth it" if the student gets the full value of the experience through active involvement, interactive engagement, and personal engagement. College is only "worth it" if the student's own motivation is the driving force behind his or her efforts.

Our primary responsibility as student affairs professionals is to create the kind of environment and conditions in which our students' motivation about learning, meaningful work, and purpose in life result in their impulse to take action. We need to understand our own motivations — Mr. Peabody's Wayback Machine is just one vehicle for self-discovery — but we also need to understand that our motivations may differ from those of our students. With this understanding we'll be more satisfied with the college experience — and with our relationships with students.

REFLECTION

1) Why do you want to work in a college?

2) What skills/knowledges/competencies do you have, and which ones do you need to be successful?

3) How much are you willing to invest in your professional development?

   Listen very loud to your own motivations and the motivations of others — and avoid confusing the two.

Five Easy Questions

> "Is there anything you want to know
> On any subject at all?
> I've got time for one more question here
> Before I fall."
>
> DAVID CROSBY

Several months ago my editor with Atwood Publishing, Peter Vogt, asked me to respond to five questions related to professional practice in student affairs. After sitting on these questions for a while, I've decided to resurrect them for this book:

Question #1. Why is there such a division sometimes between the academic side and the student affairs side? Collaboration between faculty members and student affairs professionals — it's easy to talk about, but harder to really do. Professors will often say that student affairs professionals do too much hand holding with students. Student affairs professionals, meanwhile, will often say that professors don't recognize — or care about — the fact that students have lives and struggles outside the classroom. How does one get past these attitudes to foster more collaboration?

It seems to me that the problem begins with our concept of higher education. We've artificially split up the college experience into divisions that hold no meaning for students, parents, and the general public. The very concept of division implies separation, not integration. By referring to the student affairs "side" of the house or the academic affairs "side" of the house, we've created something akin to sides of beef. Imaginary, dotted lines have been superimposed on the college cow, and these lines have little to do with the actual functioning of the beast.

Most faculty and staff want their students to succeed. Collaboration formalizes this desire in an effective partnership. Staff members have much to learn from faculty about learning; faculty have much to learn from staff members about development. Through collaboration we approach the student from a perspective of developmental learning. The key to collaboration — and other important human conditions like love, peace, and friendship — is not waiting for the other person to make the first move. Collaboration starts with me.

Question #2. Caring about students as people — really caring about them — can be quite risky. It takes time, for starters, and it could be very difficult or even overwhelming. Why risk it?

First, we need to distinguish between *caring about* students and *taking care of* students. The worst thing we can do on any campus is take care of students. They need to take responsibility for themselves, for their learning, and for their behavior. If we care about students, we'll teach them to take care of themselves.

Why risk it? Because my daughters are college students. Because most of us, at one time, were college students. Because every college student is someone's daughter or son, someone's brother or sister, someone's pride and joy. Because college students become our neighbors and our city council members and our children's teachers and our business associates. We risk it because we want all of our students to succeed, to become educated citizens, and to care about the world they live in.

Question #3. Holistic. Student-centered. These terms are used often but are rarely specifically defined. How do you define these terms with respect to providing students with a college education?

Student-centered is generally used as a contrast to *content-centered* learning. Traditionally we've focused on a body of knowledge or content that was passed on to the learner; the learner was primarily an empty vessel waiting to be filled. In this paradigm the student "consumed" knowledge; the activity of *teaching* was the primary focus of the institution.

The *student-centered* learning approach implies that learning and knowledge cannot be consumed; the student must actively be engaged in *producing* learning and knowledge. The activity of *learning* becomes the primary focus of the institution.

A *holistic* approach suggests that there is more to learning than can be contained within the classroom or laboratory. Leadership, citizenship, employment, organizational involvement, recreation, and other co-curricular activities can be designed to meet educational goals. Active, experiential learning — in and out of the classroom — provides the best opportunities for students to develop the competencies they'll need to be successful in their post-college lives.

> **Question #4.** How do you know the holistic, student-centered approach is any good? How do you answer the question, "Why bother?"

The only sure way to know if any approach is useful is through measurement. This might be heresy to some of my colleagues, but I'll say it anyway: if we can't measure the effectiveness of a program or service, it's vulnerable to criticism and the reallocation of its resources.

Accountability goes beyond the resources distributed to our departments: we must also become increasingly accountable for the effects and impacts of our departments. If we can't measure the effectiveness of a program or service, we need to seriously consider why we're offering it. If we can measure it, and if we can determine that we're successful, then it's no bother at all; it's accomplishment and satisfaction in a job well done.

Albert Einstein said, "Not everything that can be counted counts, and not everything that counts can be counted." We can use this as an excuse to avoid measurement, or we can reframe the statement so that we say, "The things we do count enough for us to find an appropriate way to count them."

> **Question #5.** What about students' responsibilities for their own lives? What right do student affairs professionals, professors, and others on campus have to get so involved in students' business?

Higher education has certain values. We have a responsibility to the greater community to do all we can to create environments in which students can meet and exceed higher expectations. Students must take responsibility for themselves, their learning, and their behavior; their motivation must come from within.

We give students the tools and techniques they need to build a life; but the students must do the actual construction and renovation. We give students principles; but the students must determine how their personal values relate to those principles. We give students the framework in which to create knowledge; but the students must determine how they'll use that knowledge throughout their lives. We help students develop and practice essential thinking and communication skills; but the students must combine their skills, knowledge, and attitudes in the form of competencies.

Much research shows that college students succeed when they have quality contact outside the classroom with faculty and staff. What right do we have to be so involved in their lives? Some would say — and I'm one of them — what right do we have to *not* be so involved in their lives?

Thanks, Pete! Any more questions?

REFLECTION

1) What are some of the things you're currently doing to break down the "boundaries" between Academic Affairs and Student Affairs?

2) Does Student Affairs on your campus care about students or take care of students?

3) What kinds of measurement are you conducting to make sure your student affairs programs and services are effective in carrying out their intended purposes?

   Listen very loud to the questions — and answers — you encounter in your work.

When Someone Gives You Grief

> "Did I dream this belief,
> Or did I believe this dream?
> Now I will find relief; I grieve."
>
> PETER GABRIEL

How well do we respond to loss and grief in the student affairs profession? Constantly striving to generate positive energy, are we less adept at appropriately grieving and supporting others who are grieving?

Probably. Loss, and particularly death, are the elephant in the living room that we would prefer to walk around, look around, and talk around rather than deal with directly. Elephants in living rooms, as you might guess, can cause a lot of damage.

For a caring profession like ours, that's not good.

My wife and I recently attended a workshop on grief counseling, set up because several of our fellow church members wanted to be better prepared to respond to suffering, personal tragedies, and losses. The timing was very good because my father-in-law was seriously ill. Shortly after the workshop, he was gone.

It's a shame that such a workshop is not regularly offered to student affairs professionals at our annual conferences: we're bound to encounter grief in our contact with students and colleagues.

In the workshop, we were told of the five stages of grief identified by Elisabeth Kübler-Ross: denial/isolation, anger, bargaining, depression, and acceptance. We were referred to Granger Westberg's tract, *Good Grief* (1971). Primarily, we were reminded that grief comes to everyone, regardless of their faith, their lot in life, their health, or their wealth.

The speaker made several important suggestions. First, she indicated that listening is the very best thing you can do in trying to help a person who has lost someone. Listening not in order to respond — listening so that the grieving person will feel listened to. *Listening very loud.* Listening to provide comfort, not answers. We can't "know just how you feel," but we can express that it must be very difficult to be experiencing the loss and grief.

In our work, listening is also the very best thing we can do, particularly when dealing with grief or stress. Whether we're in conversation with a student, a colleague, a parent, or a supervisor, we need to listen so that others feel listened to. Avoid the temptation to provide solutions or to reassure the other person that everything will be all right (don't promise what you can't deliver). Just listen. Respond with your eyes and your face, not just with your words. *Listen very loud.* Acknowledge the grief and the pain. Be there. Know your limits, and know who you can contact to help someone who's in need of professional support.

The speaker also indicated that grief could be about many things, not just the loss of a loved one (although that is the most common form of intense grief). Lost relationships, lost opportunities, lost youth, lost capability, lost faith — loss can come in many forms, and all of them should be grieved.

Unfortunately, we live in a culture that tries to avoid grief — that in some ways asks us to repress our grief and our true feelings. The sad result is that we may ultimately experience our grief later or in less appropriate ways.

In our work, we will encounter many forms of loss and grief. Grief is no stranger to our campuses, though we treat it like a stranger until it comes to our door. The tragic loss of life through substance abuse or assault. Campus emergencies. Violence of any kind. Crisis intervention requires special skills and training and, of the greatest importance, a deep spirit of compassion. We need to be sure that our campuses are adequately prepared to respond to catastrophe, however great or small.

Beyond the traumas, there are other, less-alarming losses that still require our attention. The divorce of a student's parents. A broken engagement or relationship. The transfer or graduation of a close friend. Failure to get into a competitive program or major. Loss of an election. Failure to get an internship or a job. Changes in siblings or other family members. Though our intentions might be good, our tendency (through words and actions) is to encourage the student to "get over it." Instead we should be helping the student find appropriate ways to "get through it."

It's not only our students who experience grief. Every year we lose some of our favorite students to graduation. Colleagues and friends leave to take other jobs or to start other chapters in their lives. We don't always get the promotions or assignments to which we aspire. Resources are sometimes reallocated to other priorities. Sooner or later our nests will be suddenly empty. Even we will someday retire. Even we will someday die. Before that day we will lose someone we love.

Grief doesn't understand daily planners and tight schedules. We may never be prepared for the grief that will frame our lives, but it will come nonetheless. When it does, we too must get *through* it, not *over* it.

The good news is that no one has to get through it alone. The religious community, the medical community, even the learning community — all have the capacity to "be there" for us.

Rick, a colleague and one of my favorite people in the world, was there for me, both after my mother died and more recently when my father-in-law passed away. Rick has known grief; he's a cancer survivor who lost both a child and a parent to illness in a short period of time. I remember a couple of long conversations sitting outside a campus dining facility, just talking with Rick after my mother's accident. It wasn't anything he said; it was just knowing that he was listening to me unlike anyone had ever listened before.

When Rick knew we were leaving for my father-in-law's memorial service in Colorado, he asked if there was anything he could do for me while I was gone. I thanked him, but said I couldn't really think of anything. He then said, "Let me mow your lawn for you." My first response was to thank him politely and tell him it wasn't necessary. Suddenly I realized something vital; he needed to mow the lawn for me, as his way of offering some kind of assistance. Moreover, I needed him to mow the lawn so the circle could be completed, and it was a practical thing to offer. During Rick's crises other people had taken on small tasks for him. Rick was there for me, as only a friend could be.

In the workshop, our speaker suggested an activity that helps people graph the losses in their lives and whether or not those losses were grieved. As she spoke, I realized that there were losses in my life that I had not identified and acknowledged. I grieved the loss of a mother and her untimely death, and I grieved that my children were deprived of a grandmother's love and wisdom. I grieved that my own father, in his physical and emotional decline, was unable to comfort me when my mother died, and I grieved that I don't know what to do for him. I grieved the loss of my "other" father, the father-in-law who had served as a surrogate father for nearly twenty-five years. I grieved that I never really got to know my grandparents as real people with real lives. I grieved that I lost significant contact with my siblings for several years during my early adulthood. I grieved that I'd let childhood and college friendships fade away. I grieved that I've been in the student affairs profession long enough now to lose several colleagues. There may be other, less significant losses that I've failed to grieve. Lost childhood and innocence. Lost time and opportunities. Lost youth and vigor. Lost causes.

What I'm hoping for is that I will become better prepared to grieve as I get older — and that I will be better equipped to comfort others who grieve. It's time I realized that loss and grief are parts of life, not interruptions of it.

How about you?

REFLECTION

1) Are there losses in your life that you have not adequately grieved? Graph them on a timeline of your life.

2) How good are you at listening — truly listening — without offering advice?

3) Who on your campus or in your community might be called upon to conduct grief counseling workshops for students or staff?

   Listen very loud — very loud — to the people who share their concerns and feelings with you.

The Gift of GAB, Filling the GAP, and the GAG Rule

> "Some days are diamonds,
> Some days are stone."
>
> DICK FELLER

We live in a world of abbreviations and acronyms.

They're everywhere we turn, from NYC to LA. It doesn't take a Ph.D., ESP, the FBI, or much of an IQ to realize this, but that's OK.

E.g., my B.A. in English from UNC and my M.Ed. in Education from CSU helped me to eventually become an AVP at JMU, not far from D.C. I supplemented my professional development by participating in ACUI, ACPA, and NASPA. I used to know CPR, but now I have an interactive health CD on my PC. I listen to NPR on my FM. I drive an SUV that gets me to work ASAP, and I have AAA in case I need towing in the A.M. or P.M. I carry several IDs so that I can prove who I am PDQ, especially if I wind up in the ER with an M.D. (If I'm not DOA they may need to give me an EKG.) My daughters record their favorite MTV VJs on the VCR (we don't have DVD — yet). QED.

Chances are good that you completely understood everything in the above paragraph. (If not, you might need to send an SOS to P.O. Box 1012, JMU, 22807, and I'll clarify further.)

From time to time I contribute to the proliferation of acronyms (perhaps I need to found an "Acronyms Anonymous" organization …). The up side of acronyms is that they can be helpful. Most of the graduate students I teach use them to help organize their thoughts as they prepare for exams. They're also great for remembering key concepts (i.e., "SMART goals are **s**pecific, **m**easurable, **a**ttainable, **r**ealistic, and **t**imely").

I've come up with three acronyms that relate specifically to the frustrations we sometimes face in the student affairs profession. Let's face it: student affairs work can be challenging, exasperating, exacting, and stressful — and that's on a good day! Our work demands more than a mastery of theories and competencies: it also requires passion, commitment, and a willingness to change and to be changed. That's why, from time to time, we need to step back and partake in the "gift of GAB," or "fill the GAP," or perhaps even employ the "GAG rule." Taken in order, these catch phrases may help you cope with the disappointments, dissatisfactions, and disturbances you encounter in your daily rounds.

The Gift of GAB: *Get Another Breath*

As we prepared for the births of each of our three daughters, my wife and I learned how to breathe. It's an important aspect of the Lamaze birth process. Breathing helps the mother (and, dare I say, the father) focus; breathing in and out helps to relax the body and direct energy where it's needed. Most relaxation techniques employ some form of breathing exercise. When we're under stress, our breathing is constrained, shallow, unnatural. Breathing brings balance.

When we encounter stress in our work, we forget to breathe, physically and figuratively. We lose our focus, and our energy gets redirected to unproductive practices, the worst of which seems to be worry. Something goes wrong — that's going to happen a lot in our work, but we always seem surprised when it does — and we spin our wheels trying to force an explanation of what happened, who's to blame, and just what's going to hit the fan. Although the anticipation is almost always worse than the reality of the situation, we let the entire weight of the universe fall on our shoulders.

Even those of us with the Gift of GAB need to get another breath.

Stop the worry wheel. Breathe in and out, physically and figuratively. Focus your energy on the present, the now. There's very little you can do to change the past, and the future hasn't come yet. Focus on what you can do right here, right now. You can start by breathing, slowly and deeply. Do a little CPR on yourself.

Our worth to our institutions isn't based on our ability to prevent problems; our worth comes in our capacity to address them. We do this best when we're calm, collected, and composed. When disasters strike — real or imagined, large or small — Get Another Breath.

Filling the GAP: *Get Another Perspective*

After forty years of near perfect vision, I'm now the proud owner of a pair of bifocals. I might have gone on a while longer in my nearsighted ignorance were it not for my daughter Darci. We were in the parking lot, waiting for the completion of an auto repair, when she asked me if I could read the bumper sticker on a car a couple of rows away. Squinting, I told her it was too far away. Pulling her own glasses off — she's worn them since she was about 14 — she said, "Here, try these." Not only could I read the bumper sticker — I could see billboards, marquees, and a whole world of words off in the distance. When I removed the glasses, the fuzziness that I had come to accept as normal returned. Shortly thereafter, I had my eyes examined. Thank you, Darci, for giving me another perspective.

What we see, hear, smell, taste, and feel is filtered through our own experiences. We don't know what we don't know, can't see what we're not looking at, can't hear what we're not listening to, can't smell what we've become accustomed to, can't taste what we won't eat, and can't feel what we don't allow ourselves to feel. Our perspectives are valuable, but limited.

In our work, we need to move from the spot we're standing on to see it more clearly. We need *new* perspectives, *other* perspectives, and *more* perspectives if we want to see more clearly. Seeing things from only one perspective is a disservice to our students and our colleagues. We can be better than our limited perspectives. Fill the GAP between what you perceive and what might be; Get Another Perspective.

The GAG Rule: *Get Another Gig*

Sometimes things just don't work out. I know: I'm a musician. I played in a variety of bar bands in college — everything from down-and-dirty rock-and-roll garage bands to foot-stompin' polka-playin' big bands to sophisticated uptown jazz combos. I played it all: country, wedding waltzes, heavy metal, Top 40 hits, standards from the '30s and '40s. Mr. Versatility; that's me. It wasn't for the money — I didn't make much. I just loved making music.

On a good night *we rocked*. On a bad night we *fought* (the musicians, that is). Musicians have egos much larger than their brains. If it isn't the *prima donna* syndrome, it's the choice of material (I join *The Fabulous Baker Boys* in despising the song "Feelings"); or the choice of outfits (polyester beige leisure suits should have been banned by the Health Department); or who got paid how much; or how much the trumpet player drank; or who went home with the wait staff.

Sometimes I just had to get another gig.

It's no different in the student affairs profession. There may come a time when things just aren't working out, regardless of efforts on all sides. After several years with a former employer, I finally realized that the institution wasn't going to change to suit my needs. I also knew that my needs weren't being met. Fortunately, I found another gig at another school. I've never looked back. I've had staff members who outgrew their gigs and we celebrated their departures for bigger and better things. A couple of colleagues changed their repertoires and instrumentation, making their old gigs new gigs.

When push comes to shove, the GAG Rule mandates that you Get Another Gig.

P.S.: I tried to find a suitable acronym for GAS, but the PR people from the FDA said they'd call the DA if I didn't leave well enough alone.

REFLECTION

1) When you need to Get Another Breath, is there a place or an activity that helps you regroup?

2) Who are some of the people you call on when you need to Get Another Perspective? Are there additional people you'd like to add to your list?

3) Did you ever feel the need to Get Another Gig? What happened? What might you do differently today?

    Listen very loud to the ways you manage stress.

Going as You've Learned or Learning as You Go

> "The higher you climb, the more that you see;
> The more that you see, the less that you know;
> The less that you know, the more that you yearn;
> The more that you yearn, the higher you climb."
>
> DAN FOGELBERG

"Do you go as you've learned or learn as you go?"

This simple, yet important, question caught the attention of my wife Deb when she read it in an essay in one of her interior design books.

In the summer of 2000, Deb and I had the opportunity to spend a week in Florence, Italy, with our daughter Darci. We started a tradition a few years ago of taking our daughters on an international trip upon their graduation from high school. Though Darci hadn't studied Italian, she was an avid student of Latin, and Italy seemed like the best place for her to get a little mileage out of her studies. Deb had gone to Italy at the end of her high school experience and had fond memories of Florence.

Our trip was wonderful. From our hotel in the center of the city, we were able to walk to all of the city's museums, cathedrals, piazzas, and palaces. Restaurants and shops lined the narrow, stone-paved streets, and the open-air markets went on for miles. We were able to eat, shop, and absorb the sights and sounds of the same city that once provided food, shelter, and inspiration to

DaVinci, Dante, Michelangelo, Galileo, Donatello, and so many other legends of the Renaissance.

Surrounded by art, sculpture, architecture, and music, it was easy to see the figurative explosion of experimentation and creative expression that came about in this city as the result of new ways of thinking. The Renaissance was a time of rebirth, reawakening, revival, renewal, and resurrection following a period of stagnancy and decay that has been appropriately dubbed the Dark Ages. The ideas, images, and innovations that first saw life in Florence shaped the Western World. Late in life Michelangelo said, "I am still learning." These words epitomize the Renaissance of the human spirit. Living is learning. But learning isn't required.

Some people choose to *go as they've learned*. When their formal education is complete, that's it. Don't confuse them with new facts or conflicting thoughts; they know what they know. Don't waste their time with reading; everything they need to know, they learned in kindergarten — or Sunday school — or by the time they finished high school. Knowledge and wisdom, to them, are timeless. If they've learned the basics they can figure out the rest on their own. To them, learning is something you do when you're growing up.

When President George Bush debated Governor Bill Clinton in 1992, the President argued against changing one's mind every time new information surfaces. To him, that was flip-flopping and inconsistency. But to me, the time to change your mind is *precisely* when new information surfaces, if that new information contains evidence that supports changing your mind.

In a freshman reading program discussion with incoming students during fall orientation, one of the students in my group made it very clear that her life was defined by her religious/spiritual faith; nothing she'd learn in college was going to change her values and perceptions. She was very prepared to go as she had learned. I offered her an alternative through a brief exchange:

"Do you think there's a good chance your faith will be strengthened as you're exposed to new ideas?" I asked her.

"I guess it could," she replied.

"Is it possible that those new ideas might make you think about your faith in ways you've never considered before?"

"Maybe," she said.

"How do you know if your faith is real if it's never been challenged or tested?"

"I just know," she responded.

"Wouldn't you like to know for sure?"

"How would I do that?"

"That's why you're here," I told her.

Going as you've learned assumes that you know all you need to know, that any discoveries made after your formal education are irrelevant, and that wisdom somehow develops as a result of the aging process and is in no way related to continuous learning. I don't think that's the case. Going as you've learned ultimately results in personal Dark Ages; existence rather than enlightenment. To live well, we need to continually experience a personal Renaissance.

Some people choose to *learn as they go*. Children's author Madeline L'Engle captures the essence of learning as you go: "I do not think that I will ever reach a stage where I say, 'This is what I believe. Finished.' What I believe is alive ... and open to growth."

Every day, the school of life is in session. You never know who your instructors will be, but they come from a broad range of human experience. The learning is self-paced, but there are assignments and tests every day. Much of the learning is experiential. Some of the work is individual, but a great deal of group work is also in the mix. Some of the learning is for credit; most is not. It's OK to transfer learning from one course to another; making connections between and among the different parts of the curriculum is healthy. Students must attend and fully prepare for the class of life and all of its related learning opportunities; participation is requisite.

"Life," says songwriter Joni Mitchell, "is for learning." "Learning," says book writer Randy Mitchell (no relation), "is for life."

The president of another university gave a speech on our campus several years ago. He told us about a woman who worked in his office. She loved students, thrived on the college environment, and was a pleasure to have on staff. She had only a high school diploma, and the president — though he knew the woman could accomplish just about anything — thought a college degree would greatly expand her opportunities. So one day he asked her, "Have you ever thought about going back to school and getting a degree?" "Oh, Lord," she responded. "Do you know how old I'd be when I finished?" He was silent for a moment, then told her, "You'll be that age whether or not you have the degree; why not be that age with the degree?"

I understand the woman successfully completed a program and was awarded a bachelor's degree a few years later. In the words of Taoist philosopher Lao Tzu, "Never hating, never resisting, never contesting, [she] is simply always learning and being."

Three questions for you, your staff, and/or your students:

1. **What did you learn today?** Stop at the end of the day and ask yourself. Better yet, write down your response. If the page is blank you're not paying attention. When you let your mind go over its own mental notes, it will be a rare day that you won't come up with something interesting. Do this for a month and you'll be amazed at all you've learned.

2. **What would you like to learn tomorrow?** This is a harder question because you have to be willing to think about what you'll have to do to make that learning possible. "What we have to learn to do, we learn by doing," according to Aristotle. Learning is active, not passive. Intentional learning provides the best results, but accept the extemporaneous learning as well; it can be abundant.

3. **What do you need to unlearn?** Seneca said, "The mind is slow in unlearning what it has been long in learning." I need to unlearn the racism and sexism I learned as a child and young adult; these notions were firmly ingrained during my formative years. I need to unlearn the mindset that my country, my religion, or my political party are superior to others; right for me doesn't translate to right for all. Unlearning is a significant part of the learning process.

Pubilius Syrus, in the days of ancient Rome, long before the Renaissance, remarked, "It is a bad plan that admits of no modification." The Roman Empire crumbled into the Dark Ages for many reasons, not the least of which was ideological decay and stagnation. The student affairs profession can and should model *learning as you go.* In our own way, we in student affairs can stem the tide of ideological decay and stagnation. In our own spirit of human renaissance, we can stimulate students to become lifelong learners — the painters, sculptors, composers, and inventors of our future.

REFLECTION

1) What did you learn today?

2) What would you like to learn tomorrow, and what are you willing to do to make that learning possible?

3) What would you like to unlearn?

    Listen very loud to how you learn, what you've learned, and what you do with what you've learned.

Summer Hiatus

> "Summer breeze makes me feel fine
> Blowing through the jasmine in my mind."
>
> JAMES SEALS

There's nothing like the summer hiatus.

Time to splash on some sunscreen, strip down to the bare essentials, and go outside. Here's your chance to have a cool treat at an old ice cream stand, even if you have to go out of your way to find one. Better yet, see if you can find an ice cream truck — the kind that plays jingles to announce its presence in your neighborhood.

There's a lot you can do in the summertime. Go to a youth softball game, boys or girls, and root for the underdogs. Ride a bike to or through a park. Walk barefoot in your yard. Swing. Eat as many fresh fruits and vegetables as you can and have watermelon for dessert. Wade. See a stupid movie that makes you laugh until your tummy hurts. Read a book that doesn't make you think; read a book that does. Play some music that reminds you of summer in your youth. Write a letter to someone you haven't seen in years. Clock a little hammock time. Sleep outside. Chase fireflies. Make up your own constellations on a starry night. Sing around a campfire. Take a long evening walk with your eyes closed, guided by someone else's hand; listen. Breathe.

Summer's a great time to take a little hiatus. Even if you're not on vacation or sabbatical, there are many ways to enjoy the season.

As a student, I generally took classes during the summer session. I found the campus to be a beautiful refuge. The professors were always a bit more laid back, yet attentive to the handful of us braving the overly air-conditioned classrooms in our shorts and sandals. Summer was the time for me to build up the old GPA, get to know the instructors more personally, and still have time for the somewhat subdued summer night life in my college town.

Still, I got the feeling then — and I get it today — that the summer session is an afterthought for the campus. I believe we in student affairs could be doing more with it.

Late in the spring the campus community begins to long for the summer session. Summer is seen as a time to renew, review, regroup, and rebuild. A break is just what the doctor ordered. For the faculty and staff who are fortunate enough to have nine- or ten-month positions, it's time for other pursuits — or no pursuits at all. But student affairs is a twelve-month operation, and our campuses are expected to provide programs and services throughout the year. Summer conferences continue to grow as a source of revenue, taking advantage of the widely available residence hall rooms, meeting rooms, and athletic and dining facilities. Maintenance, renovation, and construction projects are frequently scheduled in the "off months." New student orientation and admission visitation programs are summer mainstays. Student affairs is open for business throughout the summer.

Why, then, would I advocate for even more activity? Don't we have enough to do in preparing our facilities, our colleagues, and ourselves for the coming academic year?

I'm focusing here on two subspecialties within student affairs — two areas with which I've had extensive contact over the past twenty years: student activities and recreation. I believe that programming from these areas can go far in supporting the campus mission and in meeting students' needs. The rationale is simple: we program in the summer for the very same reasons we program during the academic year. The programs that are so critical to our mission from September through May are no less critical for the students attending classes from June through August. To some extent, the programs may be even more valuable when the campus population is smaller and there are fewer distractions.

The summer session offers a great opportunity for us to test and validate the effectiveness of existing programs and services. It also gives us a chance to pilot and evaluate new programs and services. Summer is ultimately an excellent time to *listen very loud* to our students, whether they're traditional or nontraditional. We miss a wonderful opportunity to interact more closely and intentionally with our students if we fail to capitalize on the tenor and essence of the summer term.

We don't need substantial funding to make summer programs successful. In most cases summer session students still pay fees; a portion of those fees could be directed toward meeting the students' needs and interests. These students are entitled to a return on their investment.

The key to all summer programs, regardless of the demographics: ask students what they want. The recreation center, the student center, dining facilities, and high-traffic campus "crossroads" are prime locations for summer programs, and programming is much more successful if we go where the students are rather than asking them to come to where our programs are.

Student development and student learning shouldn't take a summer hiatus, at least not until the end of the summer session. Summer programming is a recruitment and retention tool for the institution. It needs to be attractive to students — especially those students who enjoy similar activities throughout the rest of the academic year. Additionally, we could develop programs to complement the summer academic program and enhance its value through experiential learning. There are endless possibilities for leadership development, community service-learning, diversity programming, and wellness strategies in the summer session.

The term "academic year" is a misnomer; it's actually based on an agricultural calendar, a very old paradigm for the twenty-first-century campus. We no longer have to wait until the crops are in before we can start the new school term. We need to begin thinking of learning as something that takes place twelve months a year, seven days a week, twenty-four hours a day.

Each of our campuses is different and has its own unique constraints. What is the anticipated demographic mix of the summer campus? What funds, facilities, and other resources are available? What programs best complement the summer academic offerings? How might the surrounding community add to students' learning over the summer?

Here's a handful of summer programming ideas. (Note: The key to summer programming, as I mentioned before, is to ask your students for *their* ideas as well.)

1. Summer intramural sports
2. A campus-wide potluck dinner or picnic
3. "Dive-in" movies and midnight swims in the campus pool
4. Outdoor (or indoor) classic film series
5. A community service casino night
6. A community service day, led by the president
7. Lunchtime improv (comedy or theatre)
8. Student/faculty summer art show
9. Sponsored trips to museums, national parks, etc.
10. Brown bag lunches with retired faculty serving as visiting scholars
11. Career placement fairs
12. Campus volleyball tournament

Student development and student learning shouldn't take a summer hiatus. Revisit your summer program — and see if it's worth visiting. You'll still have plenty of time to splash on some sunscreen, strip down to the bare essentials, and go outside.

REFLECTION

1) Is your current summer program a viable educational effort with intended outcomes, or is it an afterthought?

2) What kinds of programs would be most desirable for your summer students? How do you know?

3) What obstacles might you need to overcome to create an effective summer program for your campus?

Listen very loud to the seasonal needs of your students.

Boxes and Stuff

"So you've come to understand the paradoxes;
So you're getting used to what was the unknown.
So you've reached your destination with your boxes
And the neighbors watch from boxes of their own."

R.L.M.

Mobility can be a curse and a virtue in our migratory society.

As you move through the student affairs profession, you're going to accumulate a lot of "stuff" and you'll carry that stuff with you in a variety of containers or "boxes" — some figurative and some literal. If you need to move quickly — and you sometimes will — you might not be able to carry all of your boxes with you. Boxes have multiple functions, but you should get rid of them when they become an encumbrance. Let me show you how I view boxes and stuff through some personal and professional applications.

Over the past twenty years, I've lived in a variety of dwellings in Colorado, Tennessee, and Virginia. At last count my wife Deb and I have occupied twelve different domiciles since we were married in 1978. Our lodgings have included Married Student Housing (as managers), condos, apartments, fixer-uppers, split foyers, a custom-built solar home, two-stories with unfinished basements, and our current dream house. We've lived in the country, in the city, and in the 'burbs. In each location, we've done all we can to make the house our home, and to increase the value of the abode financially as well as aesthetically — the built-in advantage of having an interior decorator as a partner!

Though we've enjoyed a variety of shelters and locales over the years, there's one thing we've never looked forward to: moving. The older we've gotten and the more things we've accumulated, the harder it's become to gear up for packing, loading, hauling, unloading, and unpacking. Sometimes, just being able to find enough boxes for packing is a significant challenge.

Moving is one of the most stressful things any of us can do, primarily because moving reminds us of how much "stuff" we have.

Our first major move came as I completed my graduate work at Colorado State University. We were excited about the offer of a starting-level position at the University of Tennessee in Knoxville. The adventure of moving to a different part of the country, of starting fresh, of experiencing the southeastern United States and the Eastern Seaboard — this was an exciting prospect for a young, childless couple. We rented a moving truck — not a very large one, because we hadn't amassed much stuff at that point — and prepared to make the big jump from our childhood home state.

On the big day, as we loaded the truck, Deb felt she was coming down with a virus. I continued to load the truck while she went to the university's health center to see if she could get something to make the trip a little more bearable. I dropped my moped on my foot while she was gone, but continued to limp through the loading process with the help of a neighbor. Our life at that point was contained in a manageable number of boxes.

Deb finally returned with the biggest smile I'd ever seen. She didn't have a virus; she was pregnant with our first child! Her parents, already uncertain about our move to a city fifteen hundred miles away, were none too pleased with their son-in-law that day. There I was, a relative stranger taking away their oldest daughter and their first grandchild. I'm sure they would have happily packed me in one of those moving boxes at that moment:

> *So you're packing up your life and now you're leaving*
> *From the only place you've ever known as home*
> *So you're on the road and thinking you're believing*
> *Somehow yesterday is leaving you alone.*

Other than a sore foot on my part and a bit of morning sickness for Deb, the move went without a hitch. Well, there was one hitch (pardon the pun): our station wagon became detached from the moving van — because I didn't know what I was doing when I hooked it up — but it happened in a gas station so no harm was done.

We quickly discovered that July in Knoxville, Tennessee, is nothing like July in Fort Collins, Colorado. For the first time in our lives we encountered humidity in the upper 90s. The university provided a house for us — a former fraternity house that had seen better days, with one air conditioning unit in the bedroom. We unloaded several of our boxes into the basement of the old house; within a couple of days the boxes were covered with fungus and mildew. Within a week of our arrival we found a small, three-bedroom starter home and put down a contract on it. Thank heavens for central air conditioning! Slightly over a year later we traded up for a larger house to accommodate our now-growing family. Once again we boxed up all of our possessions — now including an array of baby stuff — and made the move across town.

Anticipating a move back to Colorado (which never materialized), we sold the "trade up" house and got a monthly lease on a rental house so that we'd be able to pull up roots quickly. We kept much of our belongings in boxes to facilitate the move. Daughter number two was now part of the package. The job prospect in Colorado fell through. Deb's growing interest and background in interior design led to the purchase of a house in need of renovation and care. A few years later Deb's education in solar construction resulted in the design and fabrication of a home with solar heating and hot water. Shortly after the appearance of daughter number three, I was offered a position in Virginia. This time we could barely contain all of our boxes, furnishings, and personal effects in a full-size moving van.

> *You can drive your truck until you reach tomorrow*
> *You can see the places you have never seen*
> *You can see the things you can't afford to borrow*
> *With the slightest chance you might go back again.*

After living in Virginia for three years we realized we had a large number of boxes that we hadn't opened since the move from Tennessee. If we hadn't needed the contents of those boxes in that time, did we really need what was inside them? Going through the boxes we made three piles: one for things we wanted to keep due to their sentimental value, one for things we thought we could sell in an upcoming neighborhood garage sale we organized, and one for things that could go to the Salvation Army. This was the beginning of an annual spring cleaning process; instead of being collectors, we decided to become *recyclers* of the stuff in our lives.

Stuff has a life of its own and is able to regenerate itself. Stuff happens. We decided we didn't need to be defined by our stuff:

> *There are boxes made for storing your possessions*
> *And containers and compartments for display*
> *There are boxes made for hiding your obsessions*
> *And receptacles for holding yesterday.*

Stuff happens at work, too!

I'm currently in my eighth office space on a campus where I've worked for just over twelve years. Renovations and building projects, promotion, and reorganization occasioned the moves. (Many people on my campus claim that JMU stands for "Just Move Us," not James Madison University.) I've welcomed the moves because each one was an opportunity. Still, it can be hard leaving an office or suite that has become your second home. In addition to all of the packing, the work orders to move phones and computers, the potential damage to furnishings, and the disruption involved with packing, loading, moving, unloading, and unpacking, there's a bit of separation anxiety that accompanies most moves — for me, at least. I have to give my executive assistant, Judy, a lot of credit for managing so many moves in so few years.

There are some things we can never store or move in a box. The memories attached to significant places in our lives. Fear and uncertainty of what lies ahead. Friendships and other relationships. Knowledge, skill, and attitude: competency. The most valuable stuff in our lives and in our work doesn't belong in boxes:

> *So you've come to understand the paradoxes*
> *So you're getting used to what was the unknown*
> *So you've reached your destination with your boxes*
> *And the neighbors watch from boxes of their own.*

I often tell my graduate students, as they near completion of their master's programs, to imagine themselves as immigrants. I tell them that immigration can come in many forms. Some people immigrate to a new land only to make enough money to send back to their families in their homelands, never intending to become a part of the new world to which they've migrated. Other immigrants seek a new way of life and new opportunities. These immigrants are much more successful in establishing themselves in new communities. Even though they maintain their heritage, customs, and religion, they make their lives meaningful in the new setting.

I also ask my graduate students to imagine which type of immigrant they think they'll be in their first job. I then have them determine what possessions they're taking with them to the new land, and what they'll be forced to leave behind.

This exercise, done in a seminar setting, is almost always an emotional yet satisfying way for the students to prepare, both cognitively and affectively, for their transition into the world of work. They begin to realize that what they're moving isn't material stuff; what they're moving is human potential. They're not moving a collection of theories and practices; they're recycling their learning to benefit others. What they're moving is their capacity to influence the growth and development of students.

They also realize that they don't have to take everything with them; they can decide what's of value, what to leave in and what to leave out. They learn that it's possible to think outside of the boxes:

> *You can hold on to your boxes like a lover*
> *You can make believe security is real*
> *You can open up your boxes to discover*
> *There is really nothing in the box to steal.*

Moving is a part of life. We move from infancy to childhood to adolescence to adulthood to middle age to retirement — and who knows where we move from there, but it's pretty obvious that we won't be taking our boxes us with us in that final move (or, as Don Henley has written, "You don't see no hearses with luggage racks"). We move from the womb to the cradle to the classroom to the office to the retirement home to the mortuary to the grave — with countless other moves in between. Like sharks, we really don't stop moving until we die.

As a practitioner in student affairs you will immigrate from one assignment to another, one office to another, one department to another, one division to another, or one institution to another — perhaps even from one career to another. Think about what you need to take with you and what you need to leave behind. Moving is a part of life — but you have more control than you think over what moves with you.

REFLECTION

1) Are you a collector or a recycler? Are there any items, theories, philosophies, or practices you've held onto even though they're no longer useful?

2) In your next job, what will you need to take with you, and what will you need to leave behind? Why?

3) To what extent do you believe you are defined by your stuff, at home and at work?

*Listen very loud to the things you value —
and what you do with them.*

B . A . L . A . N . C . E .

"Never saw the morning until I stayed up all night;
Never saw the sunshine until you turned out the light;
Never saw my hometown until I stayed away too long;
Never heard the melody until I needed the song."

TOM WAITS

One of my daughters had an incredibly difficult time learning how to ride a bicycle. As is the case in so many other instances we encounter in life, she had two obstacles to overcome in her learning process: fear and balance.

Fear of failure, fear of falling, fear of what happens when you're not really in control — fear is a worthy adversary, particularly to a young child. Fear is tangible; you can feel it, sense it, even taste it — and I'm told our pets can smell it! Fear, even when it's irrational, makes sense.

Balance, on the other hand, isn't tangible, particularly to a child who's not quite sure she even wants to learn to ride that knee-scraping, death-defying, screaming hunk of hurtling metal. Why *should* a bicycle, without training wheels, stand up straight? Isn't this just one more cruel invention designed by an evil scientist to maim and kill children?

As all good parents do, I tried my hardest to convince my daughter that riding a bike was fun, and how proud of herself she'd be when she finally pedaled off on her own power and volition.

Yes, I actually used the word "volition." Perhaps that's why she's an English major today and not a world-class athlete.

I assured her that I would hold on to the seat of the bicycle until I was sure she could handle it independently. I took her to a large parking lot where I knew there was plenty of unobstructed space — and plenty of curbing from which she could push off to start. We started out slowly, partially in response to the look of unrefined terror in her eyes. I used comforting words and ran along beside her.

How do you describe something as nebulous as balance? I couldn't describe it, but I knew she needed it to be successful in the bike-riding proposition.

"Keep the front wheel straight. Don't look at the ground; look at where you're going. You're doing great." She really wasn't, but honesty wasn't the very best policy at that moment. "OK, let's go a little faster; it actually works better when you're moving a little faster."

"That makes a lot of sense, Dad. I can't control it at this speed, so why should I go faster?!"

"Just trust me."

How I wish I hadn't said that.

We went faster, and when I felt she was doing all right I let go of the bike. She didn't know it for a few precious seconds. When she finally sensed I wasn't holding on, she panicked. She didn't try to stop the bike with the brakes; she didn't even try to stop it with her feet. Instead, she bailed out; she jumped off the bike. Both she and the bike splattered in separate heaps on the hard, hot asphalt. I couldn't tell which of them was worse for the wear.

It would be several weeks before she would try to get back in the saddle, and only then because her younger sister shamed her into it by learning how to ride before she did.

Balance isn't tangible; flesh wounds and bent metal are.

In my previous book, *Fables, Labels, and Folding Tables* (1999), I described *seesaw surfing*, the game of solitaire I played with the teeter-totters (that's what we called them in Colorado) on our playgrounds. I recall this image because it helps to illustrate a way we can make balance more tangible. In seesaw surfing, you climb on an empty board from one end and work your way to the middle of the board, seeking the magical point of balance where the board would level out. This was not a static point; you had to constantly adjust your weight to maintain your balance. The lesson I learned from this playground pastime was that balance requires adjustment — in play and in life.

Balance is difficult to achieve for us professionals in student affairs. We constantly strive to juggle expectations and responsibilities at work, at home, with our families, and within our communities. Our personal interests often take a back seat to all of our other obligations. As I've struggled with these competing demands, I've assessed what I need to stay in balance. I offer the following list as one way to capture and realize B.A.L.A.N.C.E. in your life and work:

Bearings

Adjustment

Learning

Attitude

Nimble

Contrast

Equilibrium

Bearings. The first step in achieving balance is finding your bearings. On the seesaw, if you don't know where the fulcrum of the board is located, you have to spend a lot of time and energy searching for it. Knowing where you are, how far you've come, how far you have to go, and how high off the ground you are — these are important considerations in seesaw surfing.

Achieving balance in work is no different. You have to get your bearings. What are the various expectations and responsibilities you're trying to juggle? How much support do you have for each endeavor? What is the relative importance of these obligations? Are these expectations and responsibilities helping you achieve your goals, or are they being driven by some other motivation?

To achieve balance, start by taking inventory of your commitments. Find your bearings.

Adjustment. On the seesaw, it's necessary to constantly adjust your weight, your footing, the extension of your arms, and other bodily contortions to maintain your balance. You use many bones and muscles continuously. Standing still won't cut it for long. Periodic adjustments keep you on your toes so that you're able to react and respond to the changing circumstances of your ride. I'm not speaking from experience here, but I assume ocean surfers do the same type of constant adjusting to stay on their boards.

Student affairs work requires the ongoing fine-tuning of schedules, assignments, resources, and attention. We're virtual acrobats, frequently changing our poise and form in mid-flight, correcting and tweaking what needs correcting and tweaking. We too react and respond to the changing circumstances of our ride. To find balance between our work world and our home world, we must make adjustments. Sometimes work takes precedence; sometimes home and family are the priority. Sometimes health makes all of our other duties irrelevant.

To achieve balance, you have to keep moving. Make the necessary adjustments.

Learning. The first time I tried seesaw surfing, I wasn't successful. Nor was I the second time. Actually, it took me several tries before I could keep the board straight for longer than a second or two. This must have been how the Wright Brothers felt when, after several attempts, they finally got their plane to stay aloft for a few seconds. Basically, I had to learn to seesaw surf, and I learn best by doing. I took a few unpleasant spills, but that was the price of my learning.

Balance in professional practice requires learning as well. We may be fortunate to succeed at some things on our first attempt, but I have yet to meet anyone in the profession who's never made a mistake, never had a false start, never wished he or she could have just once more chance to get it right. You'll never err if you never try, but you'll never learn either. Balance dictates that you learn new skills, acquire new knowledge, and develop new competencies. Without learning, you'll keep falling.

To achieve balance, discover through doing. Keep on learning.

Attitude. Anything worth doing is worth doing with the right attitude. In the spirit of play and adventure, I approached the seesaw with a can-do attitude. I didn't know, when I first started, if it was humanly possible to stand on a teeter-totter and balance the board. It *seemed* like it should be possible, and that's all I needed to know. If I'd approached the board like my daughter originally approached riding the bike, a self-defeating attitude would have made it impossible for me to succeed, regardless of my efforts — at least until someone else showed me it could be done. In my case, I was the one showing the other kids it could be done.

Anything worth doing at work is worth doing with the right attitude. I can't fathom why anyone would go to work every day with the sole intention of making themselves and others miserable, but many of us know people who do just that. A bad attitude is a key ingredient in a lack of balance. If we approach our challenges believing that balance is possible, we've already overcome one major obstacle in the way of balance. Attitude isn't everything — a little competency also helps — but it is an essential characteristic in achievement, in responsibility, in motivation, and in living a balanced life.

To achieve balance, start with the right approach. Check your attitude.

Nimble. Remember Jack? He would have seriously burned his backside if he hadn't been nimble. I was never quite sure what compelled him to jump over the candlestick in the first place, but others could say the same about me and seesaw surfing.

We don't often think about being nimble, but atop a teeter-totter I knew what it meant. It's not enough to make adjustments; sometimes you have to make adjustments that are *nimble* and *quick*; if you don't, the adjustments are ineffective. Agility is a major trait in successful seesaw surfing.

I've learned the value of being nimble and quick in the student affairs profession too. We don't often have the luxury of time and deliberation. Frequently we're called upon to make a judgment call, right here and right now, particularly when lives are at stake. To be nimble is to be lively, dexterous, handy. Our ability to act is one of the things that makes us valuable to our institutions. Those same qualities come into play as we strive for personal and professional balance.

To achieve balance, limber up and stretch those muscles. Learn to be nimble.

Contrast. The basic assumption behind a seesaw is contrast; having relatively equal weights on both ends results in relative weightlessness. Contrast creates the opportunity for balance. My task as a seesaw surfer was to exploit that opportunity by placing just enough of myself on both sides of the fulcrum to achieve relative weightlessness, ergo relative balance. Without contrast, there could be no balance. I didn't understand this principle in a cognitive way, but somehow I sensed it as I stood atop the board and made my moves.

Contrast is the secret to successful balance in our personal and professional lives. To achieve balance, we have to exploit the opportunities of contrast. A healthy home life makes me a better contributor at work and vice versa. It took me several years to realize that I didn't have to take my work — physically and mentally — home with me at night. Personal interests like music, reading, movies, and gardening provide an appropriate contrast to committee work, written reports, challenging conversations with unhappy parents, and all of the other tasks I undertake on a given day. I can look forward to my work because I have contrast in the rest of my life.

To achieve balance, exploit the opportunity by placing enough of yourself on both sides of the fulcrum. Seek contrast.

Equilibrium. On my playground, I had to learn an important lesson: equilibrium is short-lived and elusive. It lasts only for a moment, but it's possible to live a long time within that moment. I realized that I enjoyed the pursuit of equilibrium as much as — perhaps more than — the actual moment of balance that I achieved. I felt just as alive when I was reaching for balance as I did when I momentarily realized it. The pursuit of balance — similar to the pursuit of happiness — may be more real than the accomplishment of balance. Balance wasn't something I *got*; it was something I *did*.

Equilibrium doesn't come easy in our personal and professional lives. Nothing goes exactly as planned, no matter how good we are at planning; the human element and the capriciousness of the universe will always play their parts.

Equilibrium is defined as the balance of forces or influences. As managers, coordinators, and leaders in student affairs work, we all have our share of forces or influences to balance. In the complexity of our lives and our work, there will always be something out of balance. Striving for equilibrium is how we manage, how we coordinate, and how we lead. When we achieve a moment of equilibrium, we can accept that it lasts only for a moment — but that it's possible to live a long time within that moment. Equilibrium isn't something we *get*; it's something we *do*.

To achieve balance, learn to love the quest as well as the goal. Pursue equilibrium.

When my daughter finally learned how to ride her bicycle, I don't know which she overcame first: her fear or her lack of balance. It probably occurred simultaneously. When things are out of balance in our lives, we can experience fear: fear of failure, fear of falling, fear of what happens when we're not really in control. Unfortunately, the more we fear, the more out of balance we become. That's why I suggest we find our *bearings*, make the necessary *adjustments*, keep on *learning*, check our *attitudes*, learn to be *nimble*, seek *contrast*, and pursue *equilibrium*.

After all, our lives are in the balance.

REFLECTION

1) Find your bearings: take inventory of the responsibilities, expectations, and commitments in your life.

2) Describe how equilibrium would feel to you in your work and in your life.

3) What adjustments could you make right now that would help bring your work or your life into better balance?

   Listen very loud to the need for balance
   and the ways you can achieve it.

Deferred Living

"Your life is now."

JOHN MELLENCAMP

Deferred gifts are a popular development tool on many campuses. Also known as planned gifts, they range in size from small bequests to multimillion-dollar trusts.

Although these gifts are given in the present, the campus doesn't receive the benefit until some time in the future, *ergo* the name. Deferred gifts benefit both the donor and the college through careful planning and investment.

Let the record show that I'm all in favor of deferred *giving*.

I do have a problem, however, with deferred *living*.

Don't get me wrong. I think it's wise to plan for the future. Savings, investments, retirement — I want to be prepared and financially secure. When all is said and done and my family's needs have been met, I'd like to have a little money left over to contribute to my favorite college and to my church. Financial planning will help me realize these goals.

I've decided, though, not to engage in deferred living. My life is now.

Too many times I've seen people sacrifice the present as they make plans for the future, only to arrive in that future lacking the health, stamina, or desire to realize their plans — discovering too late that they have no past to remember. Too many times I've seen people in the prime of life suffer from unexpected illness and terminal conditions. They don't wish they'd saved more money for their future; *they wish they'd done more with their lives* in the present.

119

It's a shame to spend so much time and energy planning our lives if we forget to spend time and energy living our lives.

Two of my children are now off to college; the third will soon follow. I'll always treasure the family vacations, the holidays, the annual trips to the beach, the week at Walt Disney World, and all of the traveling we've done together. I could have deferred these experiences, saved the money for a rainy day, and added to our financial security. Instead I invested in the love and memories we created.

A co-worker of mine lost her first husband to a terminal illness early in their marriage. She told me that before his illness developed, the couple loved to travel. On one particular trip, they visited the Northeast and Canada. The husband's aunt criticized them for not being more frugal, seeing travel as frivolous and wasteful; they should have been saving the money for a down payment on a house, she said. It wasn't long thereafter when the husband became ill. My colleague treasures the time and opportunities she shared with her husband, if only for a short while. For her, deferred living would have been a greater loss.

Many of us can think of people who passed away shortly after retirement. Some of us know people who passed away long before retirement. What do you think they would say about deferred living? I think they'd say, "Seize the day!" Mr. Keating and his students in the film *Dead Poets Society* illustrated the essence of *carpe diem* (see "I'm Still Alive" in this volume).

I sincerely believe that ours is a profession with a healthy potential for *carpe diem*. We teach and model this concept through our words and deeds. Through leadership, service-learning, residence life, health and recreation, and other student affairs programs, we encourage students to make an investment in the present as well as the future. We encourage experiential learning as a life skill worth developing so that our students can lead productive, satisfying lives. We ask students to take risks, stretch their boundaries, and grow into themselves. We're fairly proficient in training students to seize the day.

But if we ourselves work around the clock, neglect our families and our health, and exhibit all of the symptoms of stress and burnout, students notice. If, on the other hand, we take vacations, exercise, stay home when we're sick, and pursue other hobbies and interests, students notice that too. Making a *living* is deferred living; making a *life* is seizing the day. Doing both is the challenge. Don't put it off another day; start living now.

I once heard the following conversation between a housekeeper and a secretary:

Secretary: "How are you today?"

Housekeeper: "OK, but I wish it was the weekend."

Secretary: "Be careful; you might just wish your life away."

Wow!

That expression stayed with me throughout that day and has ever since. How many times had I wished for the end of the week, or the holiday break, or the summer vacation, and overlooked the many opportunities I had — *right here, right now* — to be fully alive? Was I wishing my life away? Was I a victim of deferred living? Worse, was I modeling this behavior?

My response, after some serious soul searching, was to write myself a prayer for living:

> *I want to start living a new life today.*
> *That life will be based on living, loving, listening, and learning.*
> *It will include a primary focus on family.*
> *It will include participation in a religious community.*
> *It will include time spent in spiritual growth.*
> *It will include meaningful work in an ethical,*
> *developmental environment.*
> *It will include laughter and tears, joy and sorrow, hope and fear,*
> *work and play; balance.*
> *I will ask for help when I need it, and give it when it's needed.*
> *I will be a better listener, more attuned to the needs of others.*
> *I will be a giver rather than a taker.*
> *I will engage in positive thinking, reading inspiring messages, sharing*
> *good news, bringing laughter and joy and hope to others.*
> *I will acknowledge, respect, and comfort those who have tears, sorrow,*
> *and fear in their lives.*
> *I will forgive others when they stray from the path,*
> *and I'll do the same for myself.*
> *God, help me to live the life I've described.*

My life is now. So is yours. *Carpe diem.*

REFLECTION

1) How do you attempt to balance making a living and making a life?

2) Do you have any work habits you would prefer your students didn't learn?

3) Is there something you'd like to do before you die? What are you doing now to make it happen?

Listen very loud to the parts of your life you're deferring.

Re-engagement

R.L.M.

Although it's still a few years off for me, I don't believe in retirement — at least not in the traditional sense. To retire is to withdraw, to be removed, to be taken out of circulation, to go away. In baseball, batters are retired when they're struck out.

The only re-tiring I want to do when I reach that golden age is on the wheels of my car.

My wife's grandfather is in his upper 90s. I've known Grandpa Frank for 26 years now, and I swear he hasn't aged since I met him. The last time we visited I saw him out in his yard tinkering with his collection of windmills and lawn ornaments. I told him he looked pretty busy. His response took me by surprise:

"Man is like a machine; when you stop working, you die."

Grandpa Frank may have retired from farming many years ago, but he is re-engaged in what can only be referred to as yard art. As he escorted his twelve-year-old great-granddaughter around the yard, I was amazed at how much life he still carried in a body that has walked this earth for nearly a century.

"When you stop working, you die."

After my father-in-law Harry sold his business, he and his wife moved to a retirement community in Arizona. But Harry didn't retire. He used his savings to invest in several one-bedroom villas that were rented during the winter months by retirees from colder climates. Harry served as rental agent, landlord, and handyman. He furnished and fixed the units as needed, maintained correspondence with the renters throughout the year, and managed his rentals with care. When he wasn't focusing on the villas, he played tennis, joined a hiking group, went square dancing, and participated in community activities. Even after he was diagnosed with a terminal illness, he continued working, playing, and enjoying life. Harry was living his life until the very end.

Retirement planning should be much more expansive than a simple focus on financial resources. I'd like to offer an alternative. Let's change the context and the word from *retire* to *re-engage*. To re-engage is to employ a lifetime of skills, knowledge, competence, and experience in new, worthwhile applications. To re-engage is to continue making meaningful contributions in a world hungry for wisdom. To re-engage is to demonstrate that all of the times of our lives have value, significance, and importance.

A great example of a *re-engaged* professional is the late C. Shaw Smith, formerly the director of the student union at Davidson College in North Carolina. I first met Shaw when I was a new professional. In his early 60s then, he was a literal and figurative magician. In his spare time, he and members of his family performed in a magic review, keeping the spirit of Vaudeville alive and well. In his profession, he performed magic with young professionals like me.

Around the dinner table at a Chinese restaurant during a regional conference, Shaw would start the conversation by asking a question like, "Do any of you aspire to be a dean of students? Why or why not?" A veteran of the college union profession and a pioneer in the establishment of the campus activities professional organization, Shaw was a mentor and a shaman for several generations of young professionals. After he retired he continued to attend professional conferences. Without fail he would be the first person people would see in the lobby in the morning, and the last person to "retire" at night. Shaw held court, sometimes pulling literal or figurative rabbits out of his hat, sometimes generating interesting debates and discussions, sometimes just listening to the sing-alongs and repartee that came to life late at night in various hotel lobbies.

Shaw was honored many times by the profession for his life of contributions to and innovations for the student activities and student union field. Following his passing — he'd died unexpectedly in his sleep — the Association of College Unions International created a C. Shaw Smith Society; the people who belong to this group hold court in the lobby of the annual conference hotel, keeping Shaw's legacy alive.

C. Shaw Smith. The magician, the mentor, the manager, the mediator, and the man — re-engaged long after leaving his position.

Dr. Betty Seigel, president of Kennesaw State University, shared another idea for re-engagement with my colleagues and me when we visited with her recently. Betty, a woman of incredible vision and innovation, is a trailblazer in conceptualizing and developing student success, invitational education, and college-community collaboration. Her latest project involved the re-engagement of retired faculty members in community service in the Atlanta area. She wanted to work with community leaders to match the untapped expertise of emeritus scholars with the unmet needs of the community.

What better way to employ several lifetimes of skills, knowledge, competence, and experience in new, worthwhile applications? What better way for people to continue making meaningful contributions in a community hungry for wisdom? What better way to demonstrate that all of the times of our life have value, significance, and importance?

Betty Seigel. The Renaissance Woman, the community servant, the innovator — re-engaging professionals after leaving their positions.

I'm not sure I completely agree with Grandpa Frank. I think we're much more than machines. I do agree with the notion that if we stop functioning, we die. Living is a verb — it's something we do, and it requires active engagement. There's no reason for the gifts and talents we've acquired and developed during our professional commitment to be put out to pasture when we reach a golden age. Like Betty Seigel's scholars, we student affairs professionals have so much to offer a world hungry for wisdom.

Don't retire; re-engage.

REFLECTION

1) Who are some of the people in your life who model re-engagement? Can you develop opportunities to re-engage these people in your workplace?

2) How and when will you engage in retirement planning? What do you hope to accomplish in that time of your life?

3) Is it possible to find an appropriate balance between retirement (in the traditional sense) and re-engagement?

   Listen very loud to the ways you plan to
   re-engage yourself and others.

Trains of Thought

> "There's a train every day,
> Leaving either way;
> There's a world, you know;
> You've got a way to go."
>
> JACKSON BROWNE

There's something magical about trains.

I bought myself an electric train set a couple of years ago. It's a beauty. I acquired it under the thinly veiled guise of buying it for the family for Christmas — but it is, in fact, *my* train.

The set is a replica of the same train my brother and I owned when we were children. It's a Lionel Santa Fe diesel with passenger and freight cars. Nothing else smells like an electric train transformer; nothing else looks like a 1/32-gauge train coming down the track with its headlight on; nothing else gives you the feelings you get watching an electric train make its circuit.

The forerunner of my current train arrived one Christmas morning in the early 1960s. My father had taken a four-feet by eight-feet sheet of plywood and mounted an extensive set of trestles on it. The track had a modified "figure 8" shape so that parts of it could pass under other sections. I have no idea what other gifts I received that year — or most other years, to be honest. The train set remains in my memory.

> *"Everybody loves the sound of a train in the distance;*
> *Everybody thinks it's true."*
> Paul Simon

When my oldest daughter was two, we started a tradition that is now in its nineteenth year. With money from the grandparents, we bought a Brio wooden train starter set consisting of a small wooden engine and three cars along with eight pieces of wooden track. In subsequent years we added pieces to the train: round-houses, bridges, landscaping, station houses, crossing gates, etc. As our three daughters have grown, they've looked forward to the day after Thanksgiving when they could take the growing number of boxes out from under the stairs and assemble the train. In recent years, the "engineering" has completely covered the ping pong table in the basement.

The pieces are always retrieved and stashed back under the stairs by New Year's Day. Even as the girls approached high school and college age, the tradition continued. It's my hope that the tradition will continue with the next generation as well.

> *"We are riding on a railroad,*
> *Singing someone else's song."*
> James Taylor

I took my first train trip when I was ten years old. My brother and I spent a week with my grandmother in McCook, Nebraska, an inconsequential railroad town in the southwestern corner of the state. We got to McCook by car with our parents and returned to Denver on the California Zephyr, the state-of-the-art rail carrier in the early 1960s prior to the introduction of Amtrak.

The passenger cars in the Zephyr had two levels, with the upper level encased in tinted glass. We rode in the top section until the heat took its toll, then found a comfortable seat down below. The trip only took a few hours, but I was captivated. Powerful, shiny engines. The train's whistle at crossings. The large, comfortable seats. The hypnotic, resonating rhythm of the rails. The kindness of the conductors. *This* was the way to travel.

In later years I would be introduced to air travel and sea travel. Though exciting, these other forms of transportation never captured my imagination as did the train. Over the eastern Colorado countryside, I imagined Native Americans in their tepees and on their ponies, hunting the buffalo. I visualized Jesse James and other outlaws stopping the train to steal all of our valuables. I pictured myself as the hero of any number of adventures involving the Iron Horse making its way to Denver.

"Like desperados waiting for a train."
Guy Clark

As newlyweds, my wife Deb and I took an excursion to the hot springs in Glenwood Springs, Colorado, through the historic Moffat tunnel, the ruins of several gold mines, and some of the most pristine mountain valleys I've ever seen. I first saw a golden eagle on that trip. On a train, you have the luxury of taking in all the sights without having to keep your eyes on the road or the gas gauge or the kids in the back seat.

I've ridden on scenic locomotives in the Colorado high country. I've taken a commuter train from Boston to see the witch trial sites in Salem. I've partied with my colleagues on a charter train that made a circle around Atlanta. I've toured on an over-crowded, non-air-conditioned train between Paris and Versailles. I've enjoyed the comforts of the express train between Rome and Florence, with a side trip to Pisa. Each trip had its own spirit of adventure and romance. This *is* the way to travel.

"I'm the train they call The City of New Orleans;
I'll be gone 500 miles when the day is done."
Stephen Goodman

On a recent Amtrak run from Washington, D.C., to New York City, relaxing to the rhythm of the rails while gazing at the passing countryside through oversized windows, I reflected on my partiality to train travel. Trains offer an extraordinary combination of motion, rhythm, visibility, legend, comfort, and freedom of movement that you can't find in most other forms of transportation. The large windows open up to an unobstructed world, and the sights seem more interesting than those you see along the typical highway. The sound and the feel of the train as it rolls over the rails is mesmerizing and soothing. The engineer never turns on the safety belt signal — there are no safety belts — so you're free to walk to the club car or other areas of the train. The seats are larger and the leg room more spacious compared with an airliner; you can read, doze, or do a little sightseeing in comfort and style.

"Gonna buy a ticket, Lord, down at the station
I ain't never coming back.
Gonna ride a southbound, all the way to Georgia,
'Til the train runs out of track."
Toy Caldwell

There's one more advantage to train travel. Rather than getting *there* quick, you get to enjoy what's between *here and there*. We waste so much time in our lives hurrying from point A to point B. Slowing down is a much better way to actually save time. As Neil Young sings, "When I was faster, I was always behind." The time spent (invested) on train travel may be some of the best time you'll save in a long time. Read. Think. Write. Talk. Draw. Breathe. This is *the* way to travel.

> *"The conductor sings his song again;*
> *The passengers will please refrain.*
> *This train's got the disappearing railroad blues."*
> Stephen Goodman

Planes are great if you have to get someplace in a hurry. It's just a shame that we think we always have to get someplace in a hurry. Almost every flight I've taken in recent years has been plagued by scheduling problems, delays, confusion over seat assignments, overbooking of the flight, lost luggage, and other nuisances. I'm very much in favor of safety; I *want* that plane on the ground if there's a problem. I'm just beginning to wonder if flying is all it's cracked up to be (pardon the expression). Getting there quickly has not translated to getting there well.

> *"There's a man up here who claims*
> *to have his hands upon the reins;*
> *There are chains upon his hands*
> *and he's riding on a train."*
> James Taylor

I'm advocating a new image for student affairs: a new way to travel. We need to be more like trains and less like planes. We should be teaching students to open up their windows onto an unobstructed world with sights that are more interesting than those they'll find on the beaten path.

We should encourage students to take off their safety belts and feel free to walk in a number of different directions, exploring and experimenting with the many options available to them in higher education. We should help students recognize their own motions and rhythms as they discover themselves, their interests, their talents, and their desires.

We should demonstrate the value of reading, writing, thinking, talking, drawing, dozing, doing a little sightseeing, and enjoying what's on the way from here to there — rather than just focusing on getting there as quickly as possible. Graduating in four years is possible, but that shouldn't get in the way of learning what you need to learn if it takes a little longer.

We should instill in students a spirit of adventure and fantasy. We should teach them to save time by spending it wisely, and hope their imaginations will wander enough for them to discover new lands, literally and figuratively. We should show them how to listen very loud to the trains in their distances.

> *"There's a train leaves here this morning,*
> *I don't know what I might be on."*
> Gene Clark and Bernie Leadon

There's something magical about trains. All aboard!

REFLECTION

1) Are you saving time in any nonproductive ways? How might you spend your time more effectively?

2) In what ways are your organization, your office, or your personal life comparable to traveling by train? Traveling by plane?

3) Is it appropriate for student affairs practitioners to instill a spirit of adventure and fantasy in the lives of their students? What would this mean to you?

Listen very loud to your own trains of thought.

Collegiate Kudzu

> "Been stuck in airports, terrorized;
> Sent to meetings, hypnotized;
> Overexposed, commercialized;
> Handle me with care."
>
> GEORGE HARRISON

At the 1876 Centennial Exposition in Philadelphia, Japan contributed a garden filled with plants indigenous to their country. One of the ornamental plants in this magical garden caught the eye and the imagination of the American public. It was a lush vine with large leaves and fragrant blossoms. The plant was edible and promised to control erosion as well.

Touting it as a wonder plant, nurseries began selling *kudzu* by mail. The Soil Conservation Service employed the plant to combat erosion in the 1930s; farmers were even subsidized to plant the crop. One broadcaster from Atlanta dubbed kudzu the "miracle vine."

No one could have predicted back in 1876 how well kudzu would transplant to the American South.

- **Kudzu is prolific.** It can grow up to twelve inches in one day and as much as sixty feet in one year. It thrives on the humidity and warm summer temperatures. It can grow almost anywhere in the South under almost any conditions. It actually grows better in the American South than it did in its native countries in the Orient; the climate is better and its natural predators (bugs) didn't come with it.

- **Kudzu is resilient.** It's practically impossible to kill. Scientists and researchers have been trying for decades to come up with ways to eradicate or, at the very least, slow the growth of the plant. Most herbicides simply encourage the plant to grow.

- **Kudzu is pervasive.** It literally swallows trees, shrubs, and other growing things, depriving them of the sunlight and nutrients they need. It's a climbing vine that will climb anything: power lines, houses, barns — even people if they stand still long enough.

- **Kudzu does have saving graces.** Certain goats love it, but we know goats will eat just about anything. Basket makers swear by its flexibility, and it's certainly easy to come by. Some connoisseurs praise its uses in recipes and herbal medications. If we can't beat it, there may be other ways to join it. (See "The Amazing Story of Kudzu" on the Internet at www.alabamatv.org/kudzu/default.htm).

I'd never seen kudzu until I moved from Colorado to Tennessee in the summer of 1978. As we drove our moving van down I-75 from Louisville, Kentucky, I began to see jungles of thick vegetation on the sides of buildings, on telephone poles, and lining the rock walls beside the highway. In some places this vine engulfed entire ravines, creating fantastic, elephantine forms and figures. As dusk settled, these areas took on ghost-like qualities — so we dubbed them "ghost forests." East Tennessee is liberally littered with ghost forests. They can be hauntingly beautiful in the summer and downright unattractive in the winter when the green vines turn to a deathly gray.

Kudzu seems to be creeping northward. We're beginning to see more and more of it here in Virginia. Unlike the science fiction movies of my childhood, this monster can't be stopped in the final scene by some simple act or solution. I believe it's here to stay. The meek may inherit the earth, but they'll be surrounded by kudzu when they do. I hope they learn how to peacefully coexist with the miracle vine.

Better yet, maybe we'll find some medicinal or biological secret in kudzu that will make them miracle vines in reality.

I'm wondering if we have examples of "collegiate kudzu" on our campuses. Things that seemed like a good idea or a miracle cure at first glance. Things that took over, innocently at first but then becoming more insidious as they perpetuated and grew.

Some people might see computers as kudzu. When first introduced, they were simple, innocuous, friendly. They added columns of numbers, printed pretty letters, and stored information.

- **Computers are prolific.** PCs thrive in the higher education setting; they can grow almost anywhere under almost any conditions, unless natural predators (bugs) come with them.

- **Computers are resilient.** They self-generate in the form of upgrades and planned obsolescence. Just when you get used to one, you have to change software packages or operating systems. Something new that you can't live without is consistently being introduced. Like kudzu, computers seem resistant to all but the most deadly viruses, and even these virtual bugs don't seem to keep computers from continuing to spread.

- **Computers are pervasive.** They seem to swallow desks, offices, budgets, and staff time. They deprive people of the necessary sunlight and human interaction they need. The Internet has become a climbing vine that sneaks its tendrils anywhere and everywhere: the home, the office, the church, the car, the airliner — no place is safe. We've all gotten wired, in several senses of the word.

- **Computers do have saving graces.** Goats and basket makers haven't discovered them yet, and so far I've heard of no recipes using computers as ingredients, but computers do have their advantages. Electronic mail, for the most part, is a great way to keep in touch with colleagues, friends, and family. Word processing does make it easier for hunt-and-peck typists like me to compose and edit written materials. Spreadsheets are great. The Internet provides a lot of information — some accurate, some questionable — at our fingertips. I like my computer, and I use it frequently. Perhaps too frequently. If we can't beat them, we might as well find appropriate ways to join them. I believe computers are here to stay. I hope we can all learn how to peacefully coexist with this new miracle vine.

Better yet, maybe we can learn when to use computers and when to turn them off.

Some people might also see committees as kudzu. When first introduced, committees also seemed simple, innocuous, friendly.

Get the right people together in the same room, deliberate, then make recommendations or decisions.

- **Committees are prolific.** Committees thrive in the higher education setting. They can come to life almost anywhere under almost any conditions for almost any purpose, and they don't seem to have any natural predators. Check your weekly schedule to see how much of it is pre-scheduled with committee meetings.

- **Committees are resilient.** Many campuses have committees to keep track of all the other committees operating on the campus. Some committees are designed to decrease the number of committees on the campus, but they generally realize the opposite result. Committees have the uncanny ability of being able to outlive the issue or initiative they were formed to address in the first place.

- **Committees are pervasive.** There is no phenomenon known to humanity that can kill more time for more people in a more effective manner. Committees deprive people of more nourishing forms of interaction and achievement. A committee can be like Jack's proverbial beanstalk, starting out from an innocent handful of seeds, growing rapidly overnight, getting us into trouble in places where we don't belong, and ending with a big crash. (OK, maybe I'm taking this vine analogy too far ...)

- **Committees do have saving graces.** When they are well organized, have a clear mission, involve the appropriate people, have good leadership, and have a foreseeable end in sight — both in terms of results and time — committees have been known to actually get things done. Unfortunately, many committees lack one or more of these characteristics. I've even chaired a few. If we can't beat them, we might as well find appropriate ways to join them. I believe committees are here to stay. I hope we can all learn how to peacefully coexist with them.

Better yet, maybe we can learn to make them more efficient, more effective, more productive.

What other offshoots of collegiate kudzu might be creeping around us as we speak? What other things seemed like a good idea or a miracle cure at first glance, then started to take over, innocently at first but then becoming more and more insidious as they perpetuated and grew? What other things have some saving graces but add stress to your professional life? Check all that apply:

___ Status reports

___ Total Quality Management (TQM)

___ The growing politicization of governing boards

___ Parental "involvement" in student issues

___ Outsourcing, downsizing, or "rightsizing"

___ Cell phones

___ Personal palm planners

___ Other: List____

Now, how do you turn these things into positive tools or processes?

We never know what brightly colored box contains Pandora, nor do we know what toxins might have healing qualities. It looks like kudzu is going to be around for a while, just like computers, committees, and many of the other things on the list above. One person's kudzu is another person's cash crop. The challenge for us in student affairs is to learn how to make baskets, medicine, and other useful things out of our collegiate kudzu.

REFLECTION

1) What is the most obvious example of collegiate kudzu in your experience? How do you cope with it?

2) What forms of collegiate kudzu do students bring with them to college? How do you help them cope with it?

3) If you could eradicate kudzu of any kind, would you do it knowing you might be eliminating its good properties along with its bad ones?

Listen very loud to the collegiate kudzu growing all around you.

Settling Up

"Wake up and look around;
We all stand on common ground."

GLENN FREY AND JACK TEMPCHIN

The James Madison University Student Success Model is based on three principles:

1. Successful transition of students into, through, and out of the university.

2. Student responsibility and motivation for learning and behavior.

3. Cohesive services based on common educational objectives.

To strive toward that third principle, we've attempted to create better collaboration and cooperation among the divisions of our university. As a result, I personally have had the opportunity to spend much more time with my colleagues from the business affairs areas. A residual effect of this contact is that I've learned some practices from them that are applicable to us in our student affairs operations. One of those practices is the daily "settlement" of accounts.

At the end of the day, cashiers and student accounting personnel set aside time to look at their transactions for the day. This involves adding up the money, receipts, and checks, removing the change fund, and pulling a system report. The idea is to "settle" what each person entered as transactions with what the system reflects has been entered. If the totals match, the cashier has "settled" for the day. If there's a discrepancy, the cashier needs to "reconcile" the differences.

It's a rare day when some type of reconciliation isn't required.

Frequently the problem is easily discovered and fixed. It could be a transposed number — a 1 for a 7, or a 6 for a 9 — or a check recorded twice. Sometimes the cashier must go back to the source of the data — the individual or department that made the transaction — to make sense of the interaction. Basically, reconciliation provides a system of "checks" and "balances" (pardon the puns) that protects the institution, the cashier, and the students or offices originating the transaction. If it doesn't balance, it gets reconciled.

I wonder if there might be an equivalent process for those of us who manage resources that aren't purely fiscal. At the end of the day, do you set aside time to look back over your transactions for that day? Do you assess the meetings, conversations, personal projects, and interpersonal transactions you've conducted? Do you double-check your planner to see if what you've accomplished matches what you'd hoped to accomplish when the day began? If the accomplishments match, you've "settled" for the day. If there's a discrepancy, you need to reconcile the differences.

It's probably a rare day when some type of reconciliation isn't required.

Frequently the issue is easily discovered and fixed. It could be an unexpected appointment, or a phone call from a concerned parent, or an urgent request from the president's office. Sometimes we must go back to the source of the data — the student or department that originated the transaction — to make sense of the interaction. It could be that we set our sights too high, expecting to accomplish too many things in an unreasonable amount of time.

Whatever the discrepancy, wouldn't it be good to have the opportunity to make reconciliation? What if we were to devote part of our daily routine to making sense of what we've intended and what we've done? This practice too would be a system of "checks" and "balances" that protects the institution, us as student affairs practitioners, and the students or offices originating each transaction. If it doesn't balance, it gets reconciled.

My colleagues in business affairs value fiscal accountability and customer service. The student affairs profession hasn't always looked favorably upon these concepts. The disconnect between those carrying the accountability banner and those under the student development banner has often led to separation, mistrust, and dissension.

Unless we've faced budget constraints or external mandates, it's been easy to disregard financial management as one of the less critical competencies of the student affairs profession. Student development has been the name of our game; we don't see ourselves as bean counters, so working to the numbers hasn't been our forte. Overspending or underspending have been acceptable in many divisions — and have frequently been forgiven by the powers that be. Witness the rush to spend every last dollar of the budget before the end of the fiscal year; the padding of budgets for the sake of contingency; the practice of outfitting an entire staff in T-shirts, sweatshirts, polo shirts, and tour jackets — all paid for by student fees. Stewardship hasn't been a significant part of our profile.

We've bristled at the thought of students being "customers." To us they've always been something more than customers, so we don't need to bother about customer service. Perhaps we've pictured ourselves as the old dons of higher education past, dispensing our pearls of wisdom to the chosen ones admitted to our colleges and universities. Customer service is something you get from a department store, not from an office in student affairs. Witness the hours we've worked at the convenience of staff rather than students; the hurdles students have had to jump through to change a campus policy or procedure; the bureaucratic expectations we've placed before students for even the simplest procedure like changing their address. Customer service hasn't been a significant part of our profile.

We've been wrong on both accounts, and reconciliation is in order. To be truly effective in our profession we must be good resource managers. We need to know how much things — programs, services, equipment — cost. We need to make informed financial decisions: to repair or replace; to outsource or take care of it in-house; to go all-at-once or in phases; to rent or purchase. We need to make sure our expenditures and resources are in support of our mission: to provide opportunities for students, not just amenities for staff; to conduct programs with measurable outcomes, not merely leisure activities. We need to see budgeting and fiscal management as year-round engagement, not simply hurdles to overcome in the annual budget process. We need to see ourselves as accountable for the success of our programs, the effectiveness of our services, and the utilization of our resources. We in the student affairs profession claim to be proud purveyors and promoters of professional ethics. If we truly believe in our own integrity, then the buck stops here, with us — and if there's anything left from the buck, we need to return it to the institution.

We also must understand that excellent customer service is more than just good business: it's also good *education*. We teach by what we do and say. Our programs and services should demonstrate good practice in human relations. We should create environments that encourage survival and eliminate hostility. We should attempt to meet the reasonable expectations students hold for us, just as we hope students will meet our expectations of them. We should strive to eliminate the artificial barriers and obstacles that stand in the way of students accomplishing their educational goals. We should provide good customer service so that, through our example, our students will take this expectation with them into the world of work.

If we don't serve our particular type of "customer," we may find ourselves without any customers. There are other alternatives for them.

It's a rare day when some type of reconciliation isn't required. I'm learning to reconcile the differences between academic affairs, student affairs, business affairs, and alumni/development. From academic affairs we are educated on the importance of student learning, academic rigor, and setting high expectations for achievement. From business affairs we procure the worth of fiscal accountability and customer service. From alumni/development we are bequeathed with the gifts of cultivating long-term relationships and seeking new opportunities for support. We might even be able to come up with some new game plans from the athletic department!

It takes an entire institution to educate a student. We're all in this together. Let's settle up, reconcile our differences, and hold each other accountable for the success of our students.

REFLECTION

1) What additional traits or characteristics of the other campus divisions should we consider as models for student affairs practice?

2) How do you reconcile your day?

3) Are fiscal accountability and customer service significant parts of your profile? Why or why not?

Listen very loud to the lessons of your colleagues across the campus.

The Perception of Stress

"Problems worthy of attack
Prove their worth by hitting back."

PIET HEIN

What is stress? Is stress positive or negative? What role does perception play in the severity of a person's response to stress? How much of our stress is real and how much is imagined? How much of this stress is externally influenced and how much is self-imposed? Are challenge and stress the same thing?

I've been struggling with these questions ever since graduate school. Almost every day we encounter someone who seems to be suffering from stress or the many side effects of stress. To some, stress is a badge of courage, an indication that they've got it rougher than anyone else: "Nobody knows the stress I've seen."

Recently I came across a paper I wrote on the subject in 1977. Though the references were dated, I was drawn once again to the questions. From my notes, I rediscovered three characteristics of stress:

1. **Perception.** Stress is frequently the result of *perceived* threat — the threat of environmental change, the threat of lost control, the threat of conflict, etc. We don't just respond to danger; we respond to memories, perceptions, or threats of danger. A student or staff member perceives punishment or reward as the consequence for behaving in a certain way, and this perception is generally reinforced by past experience. The threat of being punished or the possibility of receiving approval may take on significance that is out of proportion to the *actual* threat or reward. If perceptions go

145

unchecked, a person may create an atmosphere in which his or her perceptions run wild; imaginary stress feeds on itself and becomes dominant.

2. **Frustration.** Stress is frequently the result of a person's frustration, or inability to satisfy needs and realize goals. We have several needs that must be met. Often we can make sure they're met in the work environment. But if we can't, we experience stress. Out of frustration or unresolved conflict, we'll react.

3. **Response.** Our response to stress may be positive or negative, productive or unproductive. We tend to see stress as negative and damaging. But "stress is about as specific as an experience and may yield any kind of response — from invention or creation to surrender or death" (Wolff 1968, 252). The frustration of stress can lead to growth — just as it may lead to inappropriate behavior.

Stress may be normal, natural, and necessary to encourage human development; it is the pressure or tension brought about by stress that creates action. Furthermore, stress is an essential ingredient in learning (Torrence 1965, 19):

Usually it is some stress that triggers the creative thinking process and keeps it going until a solution is achieved and communicated. Stress may cause some individuals to rise to new heights of performance and achievement.

Stress is an element we can find in any environment. When we begin to understand the perception, frustration, and responses related to stress in the work environment, we will foster a better understanding of human motivation. As supervisors of staff and in our many roles with students, we must be aware of the nature of stress, how students and colleagues perceive stress, and how we can direct the perception of stress to create positive, creative, and motivated activity.

People will experience stress from threat, frustration, perception, or a combination of these elements. As student affairs professionals, we must deal with the perception and the frustration as well as the threat itself. We have a tendency to try to solve the problem by removing the threat. In reality, we may not have adequately addressed the frustration or the perception. Our challenge is to redirect the frustration, the perception, and the threat into positive responses.

I've had many challenges in my career and I've experienced stress, but I've come to accept challenge and stress as part of the work. I now realize that my anticipation or perception is almost always greater than the reality of the circumstances in which I find myself. In these instances, a perception check is in order. Most of the time I realize that the threat is, in fact, in the mind of the perceiver. Part of my work now is to help others realize this notion when they're wrestling with their own perception demons.

The most important thing I've learned about stress is that I own my response to it. Invention/creation, surrender/death, or anywhere along the spectrum: it's up to me. The challenges/stresses of a changing environment and a higher level of responsibility forced me to broaden my learning curve; the result of that stimulus has been increased activity in professional presentations and publication. The challenges/stresses of sending children off to college compelled me to rethink how and why we provide the programs and services we do in student affairs; the result of that catalyst has been a redefined student success focus. The challenges/stresses of losing parents, in-laws, and friends has caused me to revisit the things I value and believe in; the result of that impetus has been a renewed involvement in reflection and spiritual activity.

Stress may, in fact, be the primary inspiration to "cause some individuals to rise to new heights of performance and achievement." Our challenge in student affairs is to teach our students and colleagues how to redirect their frustrations, their perceptions, and their threats into positive responses. We should refer students, colleagues, and ourselves to stress management workshops, literature, and other resources — not to eliminate stress, but to effectively channel it.

Stress, properly managed, is an important building block of human development. That's a perception worth keeping.

REFLECTION

1) Can you think of examples from your own experience when your perception of a threat was greater than the actual threat? How did this affect you?

2) What do you do when your needs/goals aren't compatible with those of your organization?

3) How have challenge and stress been manifest as positive influences in your life and work?

   Listen very loud to your perceptions and what they're really telling you — and, perhaps, doing to you.

Good News

I could never understand why my father always watched the evening news (my mother always seemed to have something better to do). Why would anyone spend half an hour watching some stuffy old man — they were always men back then and they always appeared to be contemporaries of Moses — go on about all the bad things that had happened that day? My dad always fell asleep before the program was over. Who wouldn't?

> *"Your daddy's in the den,*
> *shooting up the evening news."*
> Jackson Browne

As I've grown older I've held to my younger view that the evening news really isn't worth the time. It's biased, sensational, and designed to catch my attention, not expand my horizons. Somebody discovered a long time ago that bad news sells better than good news, so that's what we're going to be shown. In a world filled with opportunities and possibilities, what we're shown is a world of death and destruction, carnage and pandemonium, hopelessness and desperation. We don't get the whole world; we get the part of it that wasn't well today. We don't see what went right; we only get to see what went wrong. I believe the fourth estate could stand a little estate planning.

"You could say I've lost my faith in the people on TV."
Sting

Something's wrong with the way we see the world. There's so much that's right with the world, but it doesn't get the coverage that bad news does. I'm a firm believer that on any given day, the good outweighs the bad. But you wouldn't know it if you based your opinion on the evening news. Give us 30 minutes, we'll give you the world — as seen through the eyes of a pessimist on a bad day.

"I make my living on the Evening News;
just give me something — something I can use;
People love it when you lose; give us dirty laundry."
Don Henley and Danny Kortchmar

The evening news would have us believe that young people in the inner city are armed, high on drugs, and ready to strike. It would have us believe that people holding public office are criminal, stupid, or both; that business is corrupt and morally bankrupt; that people working in higher education are inept and incompetent; that the government is stealing and squandering our money. Fear makes great copy. Trust no one.

"Hunger and starvation right in front of you
and the more you watch, the less you do."
Jackson Browne

There is a world of problems out there, to be sure. But the world is also home to many people who are determined to make things better, and that makes a world of difference. I don't watch the evening news on television anymore. I get plenty of news in the morning paper and from National Public Radio — some good and some bad, but balanced. I've noticed something important in my abstinence from network news: I've got an improved attitude about my world.

It's important to read or listen to something uplifting and encouraging every day. We need to hear good news (*listen very loud*) so that we can make good news. When we've been uplifted by positive words, thoughts, ideas, or stories, we're more likely to in turn lift others up with our own positive words, thoughts, ideas, or stories. If our image of the world is confined to the murder, mayhem, and immorality of the evening news, we begin to give up hope — and hope is just what we need to be effective in our work and in our lives.

Some would argue that it's important to be informed. I counter that being informed implies hearing the *whole* human story — and that's not what we're being served on network news broadcasts.

> *"We can do 'The Innuendo,' we can dance and sing;*
> *When it's said and done we haven't told you a thing*
> *We all know that crap is king; give us dirty laundry!"*
> Don Henley and Danny Kortchmar

We similarly need to change the focus on our campuses and in our communities. Good news happens every day, but it rarely gets reported. Since we observe numerous human interactions every day, we're in an ideal position to be "Good News Reporters." When we observe positive contributions, acts of silent heroism and kindness, personal sacrifices for the good of others, etc., we should make sure they're shared. It can start with thank-you notes, letters of commendation, letters to the editor, and other simple acts of recognition. We could even take out a weekly "good news" column in the campus newspaper. We could use campus bulletin boards, banners, newsletters, and electronic message boards to broadcast good news clips. We could create a "good news" section on our campus, divisional, or departmental web site.

We could also stop consuming bad news. Our lives aren't made richer in the thirty minutes we spend immersed in media sensationalism. Those same thirty minutes spent reading, listening to inspiring music, taking a walk, or talking to a friend or family member will make our lives more satisfying and more complete.

If you're skeptical about the approach I'm suggesting (and why wouldn't you be, given our daily dose of skepticism), try focusing on nothing but good news just once or twice a week. Skip the newspaper and miss the evening network news; use the time instead to read something encouraging, listen to some inspiring music, visit an art gallery, or take a walk in the park. Reflect on the way you feel following these activities in contrast to the way you feel after reading or watching the news. (Note: If you find that you're a news junkie and you just have to get your daily fix of network news, then try following it with more positive and enlightening experiences.)

I'm not suggesting we bury our heads in the sand. But I do think we should pull them out of the dirt that's dished up freely every evening on the TV news. There's more to know than tragedy, trauma, trivia, tension, and transgression. There's so much to be learned from the brighter side of the human experience — we can also know that there's goodness, grace, giving, gentleness, and greatness in our world.

It's news that must be told — and we can be the ones to break the story.

REFLECTION

1) What do you do when you're an eyewitness to good news? How could you spread the news more effectively?

2) How do the students on your campus receive their news, and how might the media through which they receive their news affect their outlook?

3) How could we as student affairs professionals help students use their developing critical thinking skills to be better consumers of news?

Listen very loud to the good news in your world —
and then help spread it.

Campus Soul Ecology

"The time is coming to do some soul searching.
No more running; no more bridges burning."

GLENN FREY, JACK TEMPCHIN, AND DUNCAN CAMERON

The *site visit* is perhaps the most productive way to gather new ideas and fresh perspectives on professional practice.

As a new professional, I visited other campuses to learn how they handled programming processes, ticket sales, contract negotiations, and student activism. When I assumed responsibility for facilities management and redesign, I visited student centers to borrow ideas and learn from the mistakes of my peers. Construction and renovation projects were a major part of my responsibilities as a new director, and site visits helped me formulate a vision for the type of facilities we needed on my growing campus.

When recreation became part of my work world, I visited campuses with comprehensive recreation centers as we planned ours. In more recent years, I've visited institutions that are recognized as innovators and "best practice" sites in student services and student success. Every site visit has broadened my understanding of the profession, given me new ideas to share with my campus, and helped me appreciate the progressive mission of my institution.

Not everything we observe on a site visit is positive. This, in itself, is another advantage of site visits — learning what *not* to do. Our profession is clearly not immune from making and learning from mistakes. Fortunately, our colleagues are generally forthcoming about what they would do differently. If we *listen very loud* we can avoid making some of the same mistakes on our own projects.

There's something else I've learned on these visits as well: Buildings, campuses, and things can suffer from depression, just like people can.

Some campuses seem alive, vibrant, healthy, and full of energy. Everything and everyone you encounter projects positive power. The buildings are clean and maintained, the grounds are cared for, and the campus is lively. Other campuses seem discouraged, disheartened, dejected, and down. Everything and everyone you encounter displays dejection. The buildings are tired and in disarray, the grounds are ignored, and the campus is under the weather.

What gives? Are these disparities the result of funding inequities, or do the people on some campuses just care more than those on other campuses do?

Psychologist and theologian Thomas Moore has an insight that might be helpful to people on both types of campuses described above — as well as the many people whose campuses fall between the two extremes. Moore (1992, 269-270) writes:

> Made things also have soul. We can become attached to them and find meaningfulness in them, along with deeply felt values and warm memories. ... We know these feelings of attachment to things, but we tend not to take them seriously and allow them to be part of our world view. What if we took more seriously this capacity of things to be close to us, to reveal their beauty and expressive subjectivity? The result would be a soul-ecology, a responsibility to the things of the world based on appreciation and relatedness rather than on abstract principle. ... We can only treat badly those things whose souls we disregard.

After we sold one of our previous homes, we were dismayed to see how quickly it lost its vitality. The landscaping was neglected; the curtains were always drawn; no life seemed to be coming from inside. The house seemed to be depressed. We later learned that the young couple that bought the house were going through a divorce. It was clear to us that the house was one of their casualties of war. Fortunately, the house was sold once again, and its vivacity has returned. The flowers are blooming, the curtains are open, and the house seems to be smiling once again. The new owners seem to have a much better relationship with each other and with their home.

Things and places have soul, not simply because we project ourselves onto them but because we have a relationship with them. Things and places can also suffer if they're neglected or abused, or if our relationships with them change. According to Thomas Moore, our places and things must sometimes be nursed back to health.

On our campuses we may find that our buildings, our grounds, and our significant things also have soul. It's easy to become attached to a campus landmark — a tower, a bridge, a waterway — and to find deep personal meaning in it as more than just a symbol for the campus. I've always had an attachment to student centers because they so vividly reflect the energy of the students who use them. Here at James Madison University, we're currently renovating a 1930s building that has a great deal of soul and history within it. We hope to maintain the qualities the campus values — the beautiful wood trim, the floors made of rare hickory, the high ceilings — while addressing the building's needs and nursing it back to health. It's a building that holds many memories, with many more to come.

It is our relationship with this building that gives it soul, and I believe the building appreciates our attention. It's really not a matter of money. Other priorities on campus are taking precedence for capital funds. But we're doing what we can to make the facility and its surrounding "neighborhood" an even better place to live.

If we can start with our campuses and our buildings — or, at the very least, the offices and spaces we occupy — we can begin to stem the tide of depression and neglect that threatens to overcome some of our institutions.

Our buildings are more than buildings. They're places for learning and interaction. Shelters from the physical and metaphorical storms of our time. Homes away from home. Edifices and monuments to human progress. Repositories of memory and experience.

Our campuses are more than plots of property with random physical facilities. They're the literal and figurative grounds for our educational communities. Places where architecture, landscape, and natural beauty come together in human scale. Harbors for innovation and invention. Sanctuaries for differences.

Our things are more than the functions they perform. They're tangible and symbolic tools of our trades. Connections to our pasts. Accessories and paraphernalia that help to define us. Extensions of our personalities.

In a spirit of stewardship, it's time we paid more attention to the soul of our buildings, our campuses, and our things. The soul ecology that Thomas Moore (1992, 277) discussed speaks to the natural balance in our environments:

> Care of the soul, therefore, requires that we see things less for what they can do and more for what they are. … In order to care for the soul of things, therefore, we must pay attention to form as well as function, to decay as well as invention, and to quality as well as efficiency.

We student affairs professionals should value things *and* people for what they are, not just what they do. We should also pay attention to the dichotomies of form and function, decay and invention, and quality and efficiency as we encounter these elements in our work. We must be sensitive to the soul ecology of our surroundings — that is, if we want our campuses to be alive, vibrant, healthy, and full of energy.

REFLECTION

1) Is your campus or the building you work in:
   - alive, vibrant, healthy, and full of energy,
   - depressed, disheartened, dejected, and down, or
   - somewhere between these extremes?

2) What are some of the places or things you associate with your own college experience? Are these places or things significant in their own right, significant because of what you've projected onto them, or significant because of your relationship with them?

3) What can you do to make your campus neighborhood a better place to live?

   Listen very loud to the souls of your buildings,
   your campus, and your things.

The Capacity to Care

"Don't you care?"

That's one of the most important questions we'll ever ask or be asked. Student affairs is, after all, a caring and helping profession. We care — but sometimes in the heat of the moment, we forget. We care — but not always in the most appropriate way.

Sometimes we take *care of* people — especially students and colleagues — when instead we should *care about* them and help them learn to take responsibility for themselves. This latter kind of caring is much more effective in the long run. The former type of caring all too frequently makes people dependent.

I had several people who cared *about* me when I was a college student. A great example was my major advisor, teacher, and bandleader; he demonstrated his care through classroom instruction, office discussions, and late-night, on-the-road conversations. I learned the value of lifelong learning, the interrelatedness of the major and minor disciplines, and the importance of doing all things well by practicing moderation.

On the stage, I learned to *listen very loud* to the music we played so that I could anticipate chord changes and opportunities for improvisation. I also learned to *listen very loud* to the audience so that I could read their mood and entertain them. In the classroom, I learned to *listen very loud* to the questions and comments of other students; I realized that I could learn from them as well as from the instructor. In the office, I learned to *listen very loud* to the hopes and frustrations of a faculty member, not realizing until much later that the same themes would play out on different campuses. Thank you, Dr. Peercy, for caring *about* me and teaching me to take responsibility for myself.

Influential people in our lives have the capacity to care about us. To care about our students and colleagues without becoming their caretakers, we need a better understanding of the contradictory meanings of the word "care." Here's a brief comparison of what it means to *care for/take care of* another person and what it means to *care about* that person:

Caring For/Taking Care of	Caring about
• Taking responsibility for another	• Sharing affection with another
• Protecting another	• Having regard for another
• Providing for another	• Showing interest or concern in another
• Controlling another	• Thinking about another

There are situations where it is clearly appropriate — even required — that we take care of someone. Children, until they've developed the knowledge, skills, and competencies they'll need to survive, need to be cared for — and cared about. People in medical, emotional, or spiritual crises may need to be cared for — and cared about — until they can assume responsibility for themselves. Some people are incapable of taking care of themselves; they need to be given care, treatment, and nurture. Some people must be in custody — in the care of the state — for their own protection or for the protection of others.

It's appropriate to be cautious and attentive in the student affairs profession. But our cautiousness and attentiveness — our "caring about" students — should lead to the development of self-motivated, self-responsible, productive, and enlightened citizens. It should not result in the development of people who must be "cared for."

There are times when we care about others too much; this "over-caring" can turn into worry and anxiety, especially when we become concerned with circumstances or conditions over which we have no control or influence. Worry and anxiety are never beneficial or productive. It's taken me years, but I'm learning to make peace with the many things that are beyond my control. I'll never get back the time and energy I spend worrying about things I can't or shouldn't change or impact. Worry and anxiety are a waste of spirit, and most of the things we worry about never happen anyway. My capacity to care about others increases when I direct my attention and concentration to the situations in which I can make a positive contribution.

To care about others is to pay attention; to pay attention is to *listen very loud*. We ultimately decide what people, events, problems, opportunities, or circumstances we'll pay attention to. On our campuses, our attention would be better spent caring *about* our students and colleagues rather than taking care *of* them. If we develop and use our capacity to care about others, we can be the influential people whom others will look back on in years to come and say, "Thank you for caring about me and showing me how to take responsibility for myself."

REFLECTION

1) Think about the people who have taken care of you and the people who have cared about you. From whom did you learn the most? How have you thanked these special people?

2) Is it possible to take care of someone and care about him or her at the same time? What are the advantages and disadvantages of such a situation?

3) Is student affairs truly a caring profession? In what ways?

   Listen very loud to your capacity to care about —
   rather than for — others.

The Lexicon of Little Things

"With a little help and a little luck,
they're going to see what tomorrow brings;
mending fences or consequences,
it depends on the little things."

R.L.M.

Several years ago I taught a graduate-level course on student activities and unions. With no definitive text for the subject, I assembled an assortment of articles, essays, speeches, interviews, and random book chapters into a course pack.

One of the articles was an interview with Arthur Chickering, the author and scholar who developed the seven vectors of student development. I no longer have the article, but I recall Chickering using an interesting metaphor as he extolled the virtues of student development in activities programming. He said that student programmers frequently try to put all of their efforts into one large program — a "large balloon," as he called it. The problem with this approach is that if something happens to damage the large balloon, all is lost. So instead, he suggested that programmers should put up several small balloons. That way, if anything happens to one the rest can still fly.

It's the little things that make a big difference — in student development, in student learning, and in life — for students and for student affairs professionals. There are plenty of big things that get our time and attention in the student affairs field — change, technology, retention, finance, mandates, etc. — but those are not my focus here. I'd like to concentrate on the little balloons that keep our sights and spirits aloft. These are things to which we should pay attention — and *listen very loud* — if we want to contribute to the effectiveness and success of our campuses and all the people within them.

And so I offer my *Listen Very Loud* "Lexicon of Little Things." Feel free to substitute words of your own choosing where appropriate:

Appreciation. Appreciation falls somewhere between tolerance and adoration. It's the approval or admiration we hold for others, the way we show our gratitude for who they are and what they do. Appreciation is our awareness of the inherent worth of another human being. Like precious metals, the value of people increases over time; to appreciate people is to honor them. We student affairs professionals should be well-versed in the art of appreciation.

Benevolence. We frequently find ourselves in power relationships with our students and colleagues. To be benevolent is to engage in these relationships with generosity and altruism. Benevolence encourages us to be charitable and unselfish in our interactions with others. To be benevolent is to be good-natured, to wish others well. These characteristics empower both the giver and the receiver. We student affairs professionals need to exercise benevolence in our human relations.

Collegiality. Where better to find the collegial spirit than on a college or university campus? Collegiality is a relationship between or among colleagues that is characterized by the equal sharing of authority. Through collegiality we combine forces with our colleagues to work together and act jointly in the accomplishment of common goals. Collegiality is cooperation, agreement, and harmony — excellent characteristics to model for our students. We student affairs professionals must develop and foster collegiality in our relationships with colleagues.

Diversity. Diversity is about variety, innovation, and completeness — accepting and honoring all that makes each person in this world unique. Variety reflects the many kinds of people with many kinds of backgrounds who have many kinds of life experiences and hold many kinds of expectations for their college and professional experiences. Innovation reflects new ways of looking at the world, new solutions for old problems, new experiences to be shared, and new worlds to explore. Completeness reflects the understanding that we collectively make up the human race; any one person or any one culture is incomplete. We student affairs professionals should work to build campuses that build diversity.

Empathy. Empathy signifies an emotional identification with another person — an attempt to see a situation from his or her perspective, not ours. We don't need to *feel like* the other person (sympathy); we need to *feel for* the other person. We have insight and compassion for the person, and we are better able to advise or assist the person in addressing his or her needs. Empathy makes us ask, "What is this student *feeling* right now?" and "What does this student *need* right now?" We student affairs professionals should operate with empathy in all of our interactions with others.

Fun. An office without fun is an office without a heart. If we take our fun seriously, we're not as likely to take ourselves too seriously. Fun can diffuse the tension that will occasionally develop in every relationship or office. Moments of levity can relieve stress and refresh the minds and spirits of people who become too focused on the issue at hand. Fun opens the door to creativity and brings out the creativity in people. In our pursuit of happiness we need to smile, laugh, and enjoy being alive. We student affairs professionals need to honor the *fun* in *fun*ction.

Graciousness. Earlier in this book (see "The Hand of Grace"), I said that graciousness encompasses acceptance, gratitude, the promotion of beauty and harmony, and living a life of goodwill. By facilitating brilliance and joy in our people, places, programs, and priorities, we teach students to act with others to make the world a better place. We student affairs professionals ought to demonstrate graciousness and goodwill in both our words and our deeds.

Humor. Medieval healers believed that humors — certain bodily fluids — controlled our health and temperament. To be in a good humor was to be healthy and in balance. We now think of humor as a faculty rather than a fluid; we experience humor when we encounter, appreciate, or express the amusing, the absurd, the comical, and the bizarre. Humor is most effective when it's used to enlighten, not to disparage. True humor doesn't make *fun of* anyone; it makes *fun for* everyone. We student affairs professionals need to have a sense of humor.

Inspiration. In my first book — *Metaphors, Semaphores, and Two-by-fours* (1997) — I wrote that the words *spirit, inspire, inspiration,* and *inspirit* all originate from the same root: *spiritus,* meaning "breathing" or "the breath of God." Inspiration is encouragement, revelation, exhilaration, and stimulation in thought or action. We draw on the principles, thoughts, ideas, people, and beliefs that inspire us so that we can find the meaning, courage, and energy to do our work. Then and only then can we inspire our students and colleagues. We student affairs professionals need to find and use inspiration in our work.

Joy. The phenomenon we call *joy* can't be captured in plain language; it needs expressive imagery because it's such an ephemeral essence. Words like *elation, ecstasy, bliss,* and *delight* can only approximate the spirit of joy; language only goes so far. What brings you joy? If part of the answer isn't your work in student affairs, you may want to consider another endeavor. We student affairs professionals should be finders and creators of joy.

Kindness. It's generally better to be *kind* than it is to be *right.* Kindness is one of the finer attributes of being human — to treat others with compassion and respect is to channel the grace of a higher being. Kindness combines compassion with gentleness, consideration, and helpfulness. To be kind is to be humane. Kindness, like grace, is characterized by goodwill. We student affairs professionals should be the kind of people who carry on with kindness.

Listening (very loud). All of our attributes and characteristics — all of our "little things" — spring from our *skill* to listen, our *will* to listen, and our capacity to *be still* to listen. Generous, competent listening is required in this discipline, and it's only possible if we're truly paying attention to and engaged with whomever is speaking to us. We need to listen as if it matters; to listen with love. We student affairs professionals need to *listen very loud* to the lessons and messages that come our way each day.

Motivation. Our job in student affairs is to create the kind of environment and conditions in which our students' motivation about learning, meaningful work, and purpose in life result in their impulse to take action. We need to understand our own motivations and acknowledge that they may differ from those of our students and colleagues. We student affairs professionals need to model and mentor motivation through a better understanding of the skills, knowledge, and competencies students need as they encounter motivational challenges in their college careers.

Now. Attendance is mandatory in life. For us student affairs professionals that means we must learn to live in the here and now. The student sitting or standing next to us should have our full attention. The colleague sharing his or her hopes, fears, or ideas with us should be our sole focus. When we're not paying attention to another human being, we can pay attention to the world around us. The smell of the fresh coffee being brewed in a nearby office, the blossoms on the tree outside the window, the sound of a student band on the student commons — all of these and other sensations are part of the soundtracks and backdrops of our lives, if we're paying attention. We don't live tomorrow or yesterday; we live today, right here, right now. It's time we came to our senses — and used all of them. We student affairs professionals need to make *now* our highest priority.

Optimism. You've probably heard of the two brothers, one an eternal optimist and the other a hopeless pessimist, whose parents attempted a little behavior modification. The parents gave the pessimist a room full of new toys, while the optimist received a stall filled with horse manure. Soon the parents found the pessimist crying that all of the toys would eventually be broken. The optimist was discovered with a shovel, happily digging away, knowing that with all of that manure there must be a pony somewhere. Optimism is hopefulness, cheerfulness, confidence, and buoyancy. We student affairs professionals should be the eternal optimists on campus.

Patience. Not everything that should happen happens when it should. Patience is more than a *virtue* in our work; its a *principle* worth remembering. To be patient is to be serene, enduring, uncomplaining, yet persistent. True patience is a sense of tranquility while waiting for events to unfold; it results in perseverance and plenty of opportunities to *listen very loud*. We student affairs professionals should be practitioners of patience.

Quiet. In moments of quiet we can think, reflect, gather our wits, or let our thoughts drift and our minds wander. These moments are necessary for our rejuvenation. To be quiet is to *listen very loud* to our still, small voices and to the voices of others. When we combine patience with quiet, we find new sources of energy and inspiration to address the challenges we face. We student affairs professionals should introduce quiet into the clamor of the campus.

Relationships. Relationships are the foundation of our profession. Through relationships we facilitate growth and development for our students, our colleagues, and ourselves. All of our people skills, communication skills, and caring skills find their place in the formation and preservation of relationships. A relationship involves a strong rapport, a bond, a link; it is our connection with another person. We student affairs professionals should foster and sustain effective relationships with everyone we meet.

Service. Dr. Martin Luther King, Jr., Mahatma Gandhi, and Mother Teresa all reminded us through their words and deeds that everyone can be great because everyone can serve. We too can be great — in our own small ways — by serving each other and our students as productively as we can. We must value service as one of the highest human purposes. We student affairs professionals should serve with leadership and lead through service.

Thoughtfulness. Thoughtfulness has two meanings:

1. **Giving thought to the questions, problems, events, and experiences we encounter.** Our best decisions are those for which we ponder, consider, ruminate, and consult before we decide.

2. **Thinking of others.** We notice others, acknowledge their individuality, welcome them into our thoughts, and manifest our regard for them.

To be thoughtful is to be considerate, attentive, reflective, and selfless. We student affairs professionals should emulate both meanings of thoughtfulness.

Understanding. To understand is to comprehend *and* value; it's both knowing *and* having compassion. We have to *listen very, very loud* if we hope to understand one another. The first half of the word — *under* — implies foundation and support. The second half — *standing* — means being upright and enduring. So *understanding* is enduring support. And that's precisely what our students and colleagues need from us. We fail to understand when we try to comprehend a situation without caring about the parties to that situation. We student affairs professionals should understand the role of understanding in our work.

Viewpoint. Viewpoint is perspective. We all have perspective based on our experiences, our education, our cultural influences, and the limits of our senses. The challenge and the opportunity for us are to realize that everyone has personal viewpoints and perspectives. We validate another person by accepting that person's viewpoint as real and true for him or her. Through understanding, empathy, thoughtfulness, and acceptance of another's viewpoints, we create a relationship with that person. We student affairs professionals should recognize our own viewpoints, acknowledge that they may differ from the viewpoints of others, and find ways to celebrate those differences.

Wonder. "I wonder … ." That phrase has the capacity to lead to invention, innovation, and imagination. To wonder is to dream. To dream is to open the door of possibility. To open the door of possibility is to explore. To explore is to discover. To discover is to learn. To learn is to live. To live is to wonder. Wondering involves the ability to speculate, the capacity to marvel, the propensity to be in awe, and the possibility to be astonished and amazed. Every campus can and should be a wonderland. We student affairs professionals should wonder … .

Xtra. Every adventurer knows that X marks the spot, and X on a map represents a crossroad. Our students are adventurers engaged in one of the most significant quests of their lives, and our campuses are their crossroads at this point in time. X marks the spot when they come to us for counseling, advice, training, support, and service. It's up to us to give them something Xtra: both valued-added learning and service. We student affairs professionals should position ourselves to Xceed the Xpectations of our students and colleagues.

Yes! The student affairs profession ought to be a place of "affirmative action" — beyond the context we've come to know for that term. Equal opportunity isn't enough; we need to affirm and confirm *all* with whom we interact. "Yes!" is about possibility and opportunity. "Yes!" is about risks and rewards. "Yes!" is about re-examining the "Stop" signs and roadblocks that have stalled the progress of our species, so that we can affirm the power of humanity to change, to learn, and to reach for something higher. We student affairs professionals should continuously look for new ways of turning "no" into "yes!"

Zeal. Zeal is enthusiasm, passion, and eagerness — all necessary ingredients for productive and meaningful living. We should expose our students and colleagues to our passion for learning, our enthusiasm for community, and our eagerness to see others succeed. We shouldn't bury our zeal *beneath* professionalism; it should be a factor *in* our professionalism. We student affairs professionals must embrace zeal as one aspect of being *professional.*"

It should come as no surprise to any of us that the "little things" are actually pretty big things in the grand scheme of things. By keeping several of these small balloons aloft at any given time, we'll be able to weather the inflation, deflation, fortunes, and misfortunes of bigger balloons.

REFLECTION

1) To personalize your own list of "little things," what little things would you substitute for the ones described above?

2) What are some of the "big balloons" you're trying to keep aloft? Why?

3) What relationship, if any, do the words on this list have with your job description?

   *Listen very loud to the little things that make a big difference —
   in student development, in student learning, and in life —
   for students and for student affairs professionals.*

Dear Darci

"Imagine yourself in a mirror;
the picture's getting so clear.
Your daughter's almost grown.
But you can only hold her so long,
'til you finish your part of the song;
then let her sing her own."

R.L.M.

A funny thing happens when you write a book like this one: as you write, you wind up learning things you didn't know. I started out with a simple premise — that as student affairs professionals, we need to pay closer attention to the things that matter. As I myself *listened very loud* to a handful of those things that matter, I discovered several more things to which I hadn't been *listening very loud* ...

What we **do** in the student affairs profession is incredibly important.

How we do what we do in the student affairs profession is the subject of numerous other publications, and the literature continues to grow every year. Never stop reading about our profession.

Why we do what we do in the student affairs profession is perhaps the most important question we could ask of one another and ourselves. This book contains some of my reflections on that question. And the letter that follows is, ultimately, why I do what I do.

I wrote this letter to my daughter Darci as a sendoff to the world of residence halls, late-night pizzas, early-morning classes, and the freedom she's been seeking for much of her life:

Dear Darci,

It's your turn now.

Your day has come. You're in charge of your life from now on. You've always had an ample measure of control, but the Darci story as it now unfolds will be written, edited, produced, and directed by you, and you'll be the star. There'll be other leading and supporting actors on whom you'll depend for cues, but you have the controlling interest in this production. I have no doubt that it's going to be an incredible story.

Your college life began today along with your independence — the freedom you've wanted for so long. Freedom and independence are wonderful things, but they're only a fraction as wonderful as what they may lead you to, if you learn your lessons well: purpose and interdependence. Freedom unlocks the chains, but purpose gives you someplace to go with your freedom. Independence lets you define yourself in your own terms, but interdependence gives you the relationships that make your life worth living. May your story include freedom and purpose, independence and interdependence.

College has the potential to give you some of the tools and instruments you'll need to lead a satisfying and successful life. "Potential" is the key word here. Good things can potentially happen to you, but they're more likely to happen to you when you're doing good things. Doing good things seems to come naturally for you, so I'm confident that good things will come your way. Potential means promise and possibility. With all of your promise, the possibilities are endless. May your story focus on fulfilled potential.

The speakers we heard today at your orientation program all shared a common vision for you and your classmates. They spoke about a moral imperative to be ethical, honorable, and principled. One spoke powerfully about what he called your divine mission to learn, to love, to live a life of integrity, and to have faith in yourself. Pretty spiritual stuff for a state school! All of the speakers seemed to be saying, *"Listen very loud, then share what you've learned!"* At least that's what I was hearing. The speeches may have been lost on some of your classmates, but I could tell by the smile on your face and the sparkle in your eyes that you were paying attention. May your story include a moral mission, a divine vision, and a faithful portrayal of what's important to you.

My words to you in parting today were simple yet heartfelt. "You know where to find me." On the surface, that probably sounds sensible enough. I work at the campus you're attending; my office is a short walk from your residence hall and even closer to your dining hall. You know I'm a soft touch for an afternoon frozen yogurt, a ride home or to the mall, or a couple of bucks to tide you over if needed. You also know that I'll still care about you even though I'm no longer taking care of you. But I meant something else when I said, "You know where to find me." I was talking about our collective memory.

I was with you when you were born, during an East Tennessee ice storm, two weeks later than we thought we'd see you; from the start, I knew you would be unpredictable. I was with you when you learned to talk, and it was clear at the beginning that you *would* talk — fast and frequently, as if you couldn't wait to share your thoughts with the world. I was with you when you learned to ride your bike and when you learned to drive a car; I didn't have to do much teaching because mobility and movement were second nature for you. I was with you when you took the family piano and made it your own, playing fluidly and beautifully as if the keys and the strings of the piano were merely an extension of your soul. I wasn't always with you — your independent streak came to life early — but when I was, I felt like I was looking in a mirror. I too was a middle child, a fast talker in perpetual motion, a music lover, a *bink*. You're blessed to look more like your mother than like me, but I can see my spirit at play in yours. May your spirit play forever.

I also know you well enough to know that you're very much your own woman. Take what I've given you, what your mother has given you, what your sisters have given you, and all the gifts — good and bad — from every person who's ever touched your life: let these gifts find their place in the person who is uniquely and exclusively you. We all are tempered in the fire of our relationships, but it's our own individuality that ignites the fire, feeds it fuel, and keeps it burning. May your fire burn long and strong.

I didn't feel my life truly began until I started college. Now I realize that the very fortunate have several lives to live. The dependence and fantasy of childhood. The trials and tribulations of adolescence. The independence and exuberance of young adulthood. The interdependence and responsibility of relationships and family. The maturity and realization of mortality in middle age. The wisdom and grace of old age. Only one of my lives started in college, but college gave me the tools and instruments I needed to make the transitions into these other lives. College is just another beginning. May your college experience be the beginning of many of your lives.

Many years ago, I wrote the words to the song that appeared at the beginning of this letter. I had no idea at the time that I was writing about you and me. I held you for a while and sang to you when I could. Now it's time for your song, your story. May you sing it with all of your heart and all of your lungs and all of your soul.

Bink the world, my beautiful daughter. You know where to find me.

With all my love,
Your Father

# Reflection Questions

The chapter in which the question appears is included in parentheses.

Learning and Development

- What lessons from your predecessors could you apply to your work in higher education? ("Lessons from the Big Guy")
- What are the lessons you hope to pass on to your children, your students, your staff, and your friends? ("Lessons from the Big Guy")
- How do you intend to share your lessons with others? ("Lessons from the Big Guy")
- What are some examples of conflicts with positive and/or negative freedom that you or your colleagues encounter on a regular basis? How will determining the type of freedom as it is experienced by the student help you properly and effectively intervene? ("Responsibility and Freedom: Keys to Learning")
- How does our understanding of student responsibility and student freedom apply to our notion of "reasonable expectations" for college students? ("Responsibility and Freedom: Keys to Learning")
- If responsibility is the key to student learning, what is the lock (i.e., what primarily becomes a barrier to student learning)? ("Responsibility and Freedom: Keys to Learning")

- What are some potential visioning and planning exercises that could be useful in helping students through their transitions into, through, and out of your institution? ("Shooting for the Stars")
- How might a student's developmental maturity affect his or her capacity to distinguish between determination and inflexibility? ("Shooting for the Stars")
- What did you learn today? ("Going as You've Learned or Learning as You Go")
- What would you like to learn tomorrow, and what are you willing to do to make that learning possible? ("Going as You've Learned or Learning as You Go")
- What would you like to unlearn? ("Going as You've Learned or Learning as You Go")

Personal Development

- What gives your life meaning? ("I'm Still Alive")
- What are some of the ways we can encourage our students and colleagues to examine their lives? ("I'm Still Alive")
- How can we most appropriately honor and recognize the peers we've lost? ("I'm Still Alive")
- Have you ever been binked? Describe the circumstances. ("On Being Binked")
- Do you or anyone you know have a strong need to wrestle — physically, emotionally, or intellectually — with challenges? Does this "wrestling" result in anyone being binked? ("On Being Binked")
- What actions or precautions might we take to keep from stifling the intrinsic exuberance, excitability, humor, curiosity, passion, and impatience of our students or colleagues? ("On Being Binked")
- Are there losses in your life that you have not adequately grieved? Graph them on a timeline of your life. ("When Someone Gives You Grief")
- How good are you at listening — truly listening — without offering advice? ("When Someone Gives You Grief")
- Who on your campus or in your community might be called upon to conduct grief-counseling workshops for students or staff? ("When Someone Gives You Grief")
- When you need to Get Another Breath, is there a place or an activity that helps you regroup? ("The Gift of GAB, Filling the GAP, and the GAG Rule")

- Who are some of the people you call on when you need to Get Another Perspective? Are there additional people you'd like to add to your list? ("The Gift of GAB, Filling the GAP, and the GAG Rule")
- Did you ever feel the need to Get Another Gig? What happened? What might you do differently today? ("The Gift of GAB, Filling the GAP, and the GAG Rule")
- Find your bearings: take inventory of the responsibilities, expectations, and commitments in your life. ("B.A.L.A.N.C.E.")
- Describe how equilibrium would feel to you in your work and in your life. ("B.A.L.A.N.C.E.")
- What adjustments could you make right now that would help bring your work or your life into better balance? ("B.A.L.A.N.C.E.")
- Can you think of examples from your own experience when your perception of a threat was greater than the actual threat? How did this affect you? ("The Perception of Stress")
- What do you do when your needs/goals aren't compatible with those of your organization? ("The Perception of Stress")
- How have challenge and stress been manifest as positive influences in your life and work? ("The Perception of Stress")

Professional Development

- What are some of the ways you get re-tuned? ("Me and My Guitar")
- In your work, do you prefer to play one note at a time, or can you play chords and harmonies? ("Me and My Guitar")
- In what ways have you had to become more resourceful in work or in life in general? ("Me and My Guitar")
- What are some of the things in your professional experience that just don't make CTS period? ("CTS Period")
- How do you model sensibility and sensitivity in your work? Who are your models in these regards? ("CTS Period")
- Does your campus have any "Bermuda Triangles"? What can you do to eliminate them? ("CTS Period")
- Why do you want to work in a college? ("Motivation Revisited")

- What skills/knowledges/competencies do you have, and which ones do you need to be successful? ("Motivation Revisited")
- How much are you willing to invest in your professional development? ("Motivation Revisited")
- What steps could you take to help your institution, your division, your department, or your office respond to the questions related to the six principles for higher education communities? ("A Learning Community in the Real World")
- Are you a collector or a recycler? Are there any items, theories, philosophies or practices you've held onto even though they're no longer useful? ("Boxes and Stuff")
- In your next job, what will you need to take with you, and what will you need to leave behind? Why? ("Boxes and Stuff")
- To what extent do you believe you are defined by your stuff, at home and at work? ("Boxes and Stuff")
- What do you need to do to improve your skill to listen, your will to listen, and your capacity to be still to listen? ("Listen Very Loud")
- Think of situation in which you felt you weren't adequately heard. What could you have done to make sure the other person listened very loud? ("Listen Very Loud")

Professional Practice

- What can you do to create more cohesive services and a more supportive campus environment for students? ("Shooting for the Stars")
- What are some of the things you're currently doing to break down the "boundaries" between Academic Affairs and Student Affairs? ("Five Easy Questions")
- Does Student Affairs on your campus care about students or take care of students? ("Five Easy Questions")
- What kinds of measurement are you conducting to make sure your student affairs programs and services are effective in carrying out their intended purposes? ("Five Easy Questions")
- Does your campus have any "Bermuda Triangles"? What can you do to eliminate them? ("CTS Period")

- Is your current summer program a viable educational effort with intended outcomes, or is it an afterthought? ("Summer Hiatus")
- What kinds of programs would be most desirable for your summer students? How do you know? ("Summer Hiatus")
- What obstacles might you need to overcome to create an effective summer program for your campus? ("Summer Hiatus")
- Are you saving time in any nonproductive ways? How might you spend your time more effectively? ("Trains of Thought")
- In what ways are your organization, your office, or your personal life comparable to traveling by train? Traveling by plane? ("Trains of Thought")
- Is it appropriate for student affairs practitioners to instill a spirit of adventure and fantasy in the lives of their students? What would this mean to you? ("Trains of Thought")
- What is the most obvious example of collegiate kudzu in your experience? How do you cope with it? ("Collegiate Kudzu")
- What forms of collegiate kudzu do students bring with them to college? How do you help them cope with it? ("Collegiate Kudzu")
- If you could eradicate kudzu of any kind, would you do it knowing you might be eliminating its good properties along with its bad ones? ("Collegiate Kudzu")
- What additional traits or characteristics of the other campus divisions should we consider as models for student affairs practice? ("Settling Up")
- How do you reconcile your day? ("Settling Up")
- Are fiscal accountability and customer service significant parts of your profile? Why or why not? ("Settling Up")
- Is student affairs truly a caring profession? In what ways? ("The Capacity to Care")
- To personalize your own list of "little things," what little things would you substitute for the ones described above [in this essay]? ("The Lexicon of Little Things")
- What are some of the "big balloons" you're trying to keep aloft? Why? ("The Lexicon of Little Things")
- What relationship, if any, do the words on this list [in this essay] have with your job description? ("The Lexicon of Little Things")

- What does paying attention mean to you, and how can it be applied to your work in student affairs? ("Listen Very Loud")

Values/Beliefs

- What are some of the "things not sought for" in your work that you've come to find agreeable and valuable? ("The Hand of Grace")
- How do your spiritual or philosophical beliefs influence the way you envision grace in the workplace? ("The Hand of Grace")
- What is needed to make your place of work more "grace-full"? ("The State of Grace")
- What are some of the ways you've experienced joy in your work? ("Find Your Joy")
- With whom do you share your joy? ("Find Your Joy")
- What could you do to increase the amount of joy experienced in your workplace? ("Find Your Joy")
- How do you attempt to balance making a living and making a life? ("Deferred Living")
- Do you have any work habits you would prefer your students didn't learn? ("Deferred Living")
- Is there something you'd like to do before you die? What are you doing now to make it happen? ("Deferred Living")
- Who are some of the people in your life who model re-engagement? Can you develop opportunities to re-engage these people in your workplace? ("Re-engagement")
- How and when will you engage in retirement planning? What do you hope to accomplish in that time of your life? ("Re-engagement")
- Is it possible to find an appropriate balance between retirement (in the traditional sense) and re-engagement? ("Re-engagement")
- What do you do when you're an eyewitness to good news? How could you spread the news more effectively? ("Good News")
- How do the students on your campus receive their news, and how might the media through which they receive their news affect their outlook? ("Good News")
- How could we as student affairs professionals help students use their developing critical thinking skills to be better consumers of news? ("Good News")

- Is your campus or the building you work in: a) alive, vibrant, healthy, and full of energy; b) depressed, disheartened, dejected, and down; or c) somewhere between these extremes? ("Campus Soul Ecology")
- What are some of the places or things you associate with your own college experience? Are these places or things significant in their own right, significant because of what you've projected onto them, or significant because of your relationship with them? ("Campus Soul Ecology")
- What can you do to make your campus neighborhood a better place to live? ("Campus Soul Ecology")
- Think about the people who have taken care of you and the people who have cared about you. From whom did you learn the most? How have you thanked these special people? ("The Capacity to Care")
- Is it possible to take care of someone and care about him or her at the same time? What are the advantages and disadvantages of such a situation? ("The Capacity to Care")
- Is student affairs truly a caring profession? In what ways? ("The Capacity to Care")
- How educationally purposeful is our campus? Are all programs, services, and activities based on educational objectives? Is collaboration expected or merely encouraged? Do students understand the connections among various classes and between their curricular and co-curricular programs? Do we have an ethos of excellence and scholarship, or one of activity and stimulation? Are we an educationally purposeful community? ("A Learning Community in the Real World")
- How open is our campus? Do all people experience a sense of freedom here, or is freedom based on power? Is civility the rule of thumb, or is it a rule to be enforced? Is freedom a special privilege for some community members and not for others (e.g., academic freedom for faculty but not others)? Are people free to do whatever they want, or are there boundaries to freedom? Are we an open community? ("A Learning Community in the Real World")
- How just is our campus? What role does fairness play in assignments, grading, and decision making? Does justice mean treating everyone the same? Is justice more important than compassion? Does the majority always rule? What

consideration is given to individual differences and needs? Are we a just community? ("A Learning Community in the Real World")

- How disciplined is our campus? When do community interests and the common good take precedence over individual interests? Do all members of the community understand their civic responsibilities to the rest of the community? Are campus expectations reasonable and appropriate? What does it mean to be a good citizen? How does the campus handle disturbances and inappropriate behavior? Are we a disciplined community? ("A Learning Community in the Real World")

- How caring is our campus? How do we respond to individual and group crises? Does our campus have any physical, psychological, social, or economic barriers that make it impossible for some people to succeed here? Do student needs drive budgets, or is it vice versa? Do the people who work here like each other? How do we handle staff concerns? Are we a caring community? ("A Learning Community in the Real World")

- How celebrative is our campus? What traditions, rituals, ceremonies, and practices define us as a community? How do we celebrate the transitions of all members of our community into, through, and out of the institution? What do we honor and why? How do we celebrate diversity and unity simultaneously? Who are our heroes and heroines? What are our symbols? Are we a celebrative community? ("A Learning Community in the Real World")

Resources

AAHE, ACPA, and NASPA. 1998. *Joint task force on student learning: Draft position paper.* March. Available at www.acpa.nche.edu/tskfrce/joint.htm.

Autry, James A. 1991. *Love and profit: The art of caring leadership.* New York: Avon Books.

Berlin, Isaiah. 1970. *Four essays on liberty.* New York: Oxford Press.

Campbell, Joseph. 1991. *The power of myth.* New York: Anchor Books.

Canfield, Jack and Frank Siccone. 1995. *101 ways to develop student self-esteem and responsibility.* Boston: Allyn & Bacon.

Carnegie Foundation for the Advancement of Teaching. 1990. *Campus life: In search of community.* Lawrenceville, NJ: Princeton University Press.

Cavanaugh, James. 1990. *The sower's seeds: One hundred inspiring stories for preaching, teaching, and public speaking.* Mahwah, NJ: Paulist Press.

Davis, Todd M. and Patricia Hillman Murrell. 1993. *Turning teaching into learning: The role of student responsibility in the collegiate experience.* ASHE-ERIC Higher Education Report No. 8. Washington, DC: School of Education and Human Development, George Washington University.

Davis Kasl, Charlotte.1995. *Finding joy.* New York: Harper-Perennial.

Dowdall, Joyce. 2000. Creativity that lasts. In *Spirituality and health*, by Deirdre Taylor. Generative Leadership Group: Somerville, NJ.

Estanek, Sandra M. 1995. Definitions of freedom and their student affairs application: A matrix for decision-making. *NASPA Journal*, 33(1): 65-71.

Hersey, Paul and Kenneth Blanchard. 1985. *Situational leader.* New York: Warner.

McMillan, James H. and Donelson R. Forsythe. 1991. What theories of motivation say about why learners learn. In *College teaching: From theory to practice,* edited by Robert J. Menges and Marilla D. Svincki. New Directions for Teaching and Learning No. 45. San Francisco: Jossey-Bass, Publishers.

McNamara, William. 1981. *Christian mysticism.* New York: Continuum Publishing Company.

Mitchell, Randy L. 1987. Control your destiny by planning work-flow process. *ACUI Bulletin,* May: 9-11.

Mitchell, Randy L. 1997. *Metaphors, semaphores, and two-by-fours.* Bloomington, IN: Association of College Unions International.

Mitchell, Randy L. 1999. *Fables, labels, and folding tables.* Madison, WI: Atwood Publishing.

Moore, Thomas. 1992. *Care of the soul.* New York: HarperCollins.

Pace, C. Robert. 1984. *Measuring the quality of college student experiences.* Los Angeles: UCLA Center for the Study of Evaluation.

Peck, M. Scott. 1997. *The road less traveled and beyond: Spiritual growth in an age of anxiety.* New York: Simon and Schuster.

Torrence, E. Paul. 1965. *Constructive behavior: Stress, personalilty, and mental health.* Belmont, CA: Wadsworth Publishing.

Westberg, Granger. 1971. *Good grief.* Minneapolis: Fortress Press.

Wolff, Harold G. 1968. *Stress and disease.* 2nd edition. Springfield, IL: Thomas Books.

Yankelovich, Daniel. 1981. *New rules: Searching for self-fulfillment in a world turned upside down.* New York: Bantam.

Randy L. Mitchell is Associate Vice President for Student Success Programs at James Madison University in Harrisonburg, Virginia. His current responsibilities include development of the Student Success Learning Center, the Student Success Service Center, and the Student Success Welcome Center. He oversees several university departments, including admissions, advising, disability services, service-learning, and first-year programs. Most of his professional time is spent pursuing the three P's: *performance* improvement, *process* improvement, and *place* improvement.

Prior to his current assignment, Randy served as Acting Associate Vice President for Enrollment Services (1996-1997), Director of the James Madison University Center (1987-1996), and Assistant Professor of Psychology (1987-present). Prior to his work at James Madison, Randy served as Program Advisor, Assistant Director, and Associate Director of the Carolyn P. Brown Memorial Union at the University of Tennessee (1978-1987).

Randy has a B.A. in English from the University of Northern Colorado (1976) and an M.Ed. in College Student Personnel Administration from Colorado State University (1978). He has worked with student activities, recreation, university centers, leadership development, student media, financial aid, registra-tion/records, and student employment, and he has been involved with numerous construction projects related to these programs.

Randy has published widely and has conducted numerous presentations on student success, leadership development, service-learning, organizational change, facilities planning and management, role theory, and student employment. The

Association of College Unions International published his first book, *Metaphors, Semaphores, and Two-by-fours: Reflections on a Personal Profession,* in 1997. Atwood Publishing released his second book, *Fables, Labels, and Folding Tables: Reflections on the Student Affairs Profession,* in 1999.

Randy has been honored by the Virginia Association of Student Personnel Administrators (Outstanding Professional, 2000); the Association of College Unions International (Recognition for Dedication to the Profession, 1999; Chester A. Berry Scholar Award for Excellence in Writing, 1992); and Outstanding Young Men of America (1989).

Randy and his wife Deb are the proud parents of three daughters and two cats. Randy's extracurricular interests include music (performing, recording, and *listening very loud*), making salsa, public speaking, and enjoying the good life in the Shenandoah Valley.